~ All Are Chosen

∼ All Are Chosen

Stories of Lay Ministry and Leadership

Edited by Margaret L. Beard
and Roger W. Comstock

Skinner House Books
Boston

Copyright © 1998 by the Unitarian Universalist Association,
25 Beacon Street, Boston, MA 02108-2800. All rights reserved.

Printed in the USA.

Text and cover design by Suzanne Morgan.
Cover illustration by Patricia Frevert.

ISBN 1-55896-360-X

10 9 8 7 6 5 4 3 2
05 04 03 02 01 00 99 98

To Rick and Faith
with love and thanks

Contents

⌣ Serving Many Well

⌣ Serving in the Wider World

～ All Are Chosen

Introduction

These are stories of lay ministry and lay leadership that are happening in our churches in both small and large ways, through informal and formal arrangements. Our authors vary in background and temperament. They represent all ages from the early twenties to the seventies, and a variety of races and cultures. Most are volunteers, some are paid. We are grateful to all of them. They lead busy lives—lives made richer by their lay ministry and leadership. We hope you find a bit of your story here or perhaps an invitation to try something new.

In our work we have seen a trend toward empowering the congregation's members to social action on the local level, and we have seen an increasing tendency in our churches to permit the laity to do the work of the church: to minister to each other; to reach out and help someone, whether inside or outside the congregation; to "find a hurt and heal it." A great part of the recent call to spirituality in our churches can be attributed to this urge to service coming from our members.

The title *All Are Chosen: Stories of Lay Ministry and Leadership* grew out of the root word for *laity*, the ancient Greek word *laos*. It means "the chosen people." All too often now the word *laity* has the connotation of "not quite as good" or "not professional." How far our understanding of laity has grown from the original meaning! While much of the lay ministry and leadership is done on a volunteer basis, some laypeople do church work professionally even though they are not ordained. And whether the ministry/leadership is paid or volunteer, everyone's goals should be professional in terms of quality. The use of the word *all* in our title fits well with our Universalist roots. "All," not just "some," are chosen for lay ministry and leadership. Our congregations, our members, and the wider world need and deserve the best we can offer. And they need all of us!

Margaret L. Beard
Extension Ministry Director
Department for
   Congregational, District,
   and Extension Services
Unitarian Universalist Association

Roger W. Comstock
District Executive
Thomas Jefferson District
Unitarian Universalist Association

~ Learning to Serve

Congregations as Seminary for the Laity

Beverly Smrha

We are united and defined by how we live our daily lives as Unitarian Universalists—how we act as citizens in the world, and how we relate to our families, our coworkers, and the children in our communities. To live such lives, we need the support and encouragement of our congregations. There we develop our abilities to connect with the deepest core of our being, and to live our lives in accord with what is of most value to us. Our congregations can act as seminaries for the laity.

This is the story of how one church developed a lay ministry program, as well as an education and certification process to ensure its excellence. It is the story of a worship committee, which then developed a worship associates program, which in turn became the first component of the lay ministry program at the First Unitarian Church of Oakland, California. It is the story of a congregation's transformation from expecting to be served *by* the ordained ministers to welcoming meaningful opportunities to serve *along with* the ordained ministers. We call it Shared Ministry.

Our congregation had become very small. The church had a glorious history and many fond memories of being a vibrant congregation. But our building was in bad shape, located in a downtown area that had deteriorated. The leadership had just called a new minister, an Urban Extension Minister, who had the capacity for bold leadership and had a vision of congregational collaboration.

Slowly, the congregation began to grow in numbers, partly because of the quality of the worship services. The sermons and readings spoke to the realities and the aspirations of a people eager to live life with a commitment to meaning. Worship became the heart and soul of our congregation's ministry and of the church's revitalization. From within this small and slowly growing congregation, a few people surfaced that were eager for even more lay involvement in worship. We knew that a richer and more varied liturgy can be possible when more people bring their special gifts to the design and celebration of worship. We began with a simple agenda: to add our energies and talents to the weekly worship service. It was awesome to even consider becoming a worship leader within this community. For worship to be effective, there must be a high degree of trust between the congregant and the worship leader. And that trust must be earned through the development of appropriate skills.

We were a few layfolk who didn't yet have the language to articulate where we were headed. This was the early

1980s and we did not know of others who were also doing this work. But we were working with an ordained minister who understood that excellent worship was the core of a healthy and flourishing church life, a minister who was willing and eager to share the responsibility and authority of leading worship if we were willing to accept some challenges. Were we willing to take this work seriously enough to make the commitment to sufficient preliminary training? Were we willing to continue to develop the art as well as the scholarship of worship? Were we willing to invest ourselves fully in this responsibility? Were we willing to aspire to and work toward excellence?

We began our education about worship and worship design with an all-day retreat which utilized resources from within and from outside the congregation. We learned about worship theory, worship design, and lay-clergy worship possibilities. We practiced the art of worship and then discussed what we had experienced. We began to learn how to talk about the worship experience, worship design, and liturgical styles. We began to realize just how large was this body of knowledge that we were venturing to become familiar with. We constituted ourselves as the "worship committee."

We started on this journey of development by agreeing to keep our communications open and clear. We shared our hopes and our fears honestly. We became accountable to each other as a step toward being accountable to the church. Talking the truth in love was the bedrock of this growing collaborative relationship. We moved slowly and sensitively.

As the worship committee, we began to experiment with various liturgical components. We explored the theories behind them so that we could design practices that were useful to our church's culture and style. We were gentle with the congregation and they were gentle, usually, with us. We stretched but we did not shock. We tested, we modified, we changed the order, we tried, we listened. Over approximately two years, we developed the liturgy for the church's worship service, which stands almost unchanged a decade later.

As we developed our knowledge and our self-confidence, most of the committee members began to actively participate in leading worship—actually getting up in the chancel on Sunday and doing it. It seemed so radical at the time. At first our role was to read one of the two readings that the minister had chosen, the minister reading the other. As we further developed the liturgy, we began to lead these new portions of the service as well.

After a few months, we began to understand that the worship conversation had broadened. Worship services had become active and public conversations among the liturgist (the lay member of the worship committee), the preacher (usually the ordained minister), and the worshiping congregation. Engagement with the worship services had been very high; it became even more so.

Slowly the worship committee began to realize there was a next step. We had successfully developed a core group of talented and committed folks, but we were only a very few. We wanted the congregation as a whole to fully understand the craft of worship, to feel fully participatory in the act of worship. We wanted the congregation to have the experience of leading worship so that their participation, while sitting in the pews on an average Sunday, would be different, deeper, and more demanding.

We began to design what came to be known as the worship associates program. We wanted to rotate congregation members through a process of learning and doing, and then resting from that doing. We wanted to include a broad representation of the people who were actively engaged in the life of the congregation—the committees and interest groups, lifestyles, ages, length of membership. We wanted the participants in this program to bring the full life of the church into their leading of worship. Above all, we knew that this program must expect and require excellence. Being a worship associate would be a sacred honor and responsibility.

We envisioned a process in which a few members would covenant with the full congregation. The promise would be to learn and practice, to be willing to develop fully one's ability to do the work, to accept the opportunity to plumb the depths of our souls, to work in collaborative partnership with the ordained clergy, and to accept the awesome honor and power of leading worship.

We designed a fairly simple worship associates application, complete with explanations and deadlines. The worship committee and the ministers would select the associates, twelve people to serve one-year terms. Each of the twelve would actively participate in two or three services that year.

11

Though the congregation welcomed the program, there was some discomfort with the concept of a selected rather than an open group. Most of our committees are open to all. Wasn't this creating an elite? The worship committee took the opportunity to discuss more fully with the congregation the theoretical basis to our vision. The conversation was productive and useful. In the end the congregation generally supported this new way of working.

During the first couple of years, the program grew slowly and steadily. The purpose of the associates was two-fold: to learn how to become an excellent worship leader and to demonstrate that laypeople could indeed do this work well. The role was that of liturgist, to lead most of the segments of the order of service. The choice of the theme for the day, the subject of the sermon or homily, was still the responsibility of the preacher, usually an ordained minister.

The education and certification of this lay ministry program is based on the seminary model. Some education is in formal educational sessions, and much is informal and spread throughout congregational life.

Shortly after the selection process is complete, a retreat is held that is at least a full day, preferably twenty-four hours in length. The retreat attempts to balance instruction with praxis. Some workshops cover concrete topics such as the history of our church's liturgy, crafting calls to worship, and creating introductions to meditations. Other workshops address more philosophical issues such as freedom of the pulpit and the source of one's authority. The workshops involve many opportunities to practice and experience worship, from composing a grace before meals to designing a ten-minute worship service in twenty minutes with two other people.

In addition to the retreat, instruction in voicework and choreography is provided for the associates. Developing these "staging" skills is important so that the worship leader can be free from unduly focusing on them during a worship service, and can be free to focus on the messages that are being shared.

Most of the educational process takes place informally. By observing the variety of styles and the constancy of excellence that previous associates have brought to the worship experience, we learn much of what is expected of us. We observe how the associates engage in the various aspects of church life, how they bring that engagement to worship, how they bring their worship-leading experience back into the committee life of the church. We learn by listening hard and watching closely, talking about and reflecting deeply.

After the associates program had been operating for a time and had gained credibility, the ordained ministers proposed a bold change. They proposed that the worship associates constitute a decision-making group that would join with the ministers in choosing the theme for the day, the subject of the sermon.

At this point, the role of the associates expanded to the form it has today. The associates meet with the ministers and the music director three times a year. Together they decide on the worship calendar for the coming months, then assign responsibilities and agree on working relationships. A minister and an associate agree to work on a particular issue for a particular day. They each research the issue and search out appropriate readings and music. The ministers preach on issues that they are convinced are worthwhile and that they have something worthwhile to say about.

The congregation certifies the worship associates in a service we have come to call "Investiture of the Associates." As a symbolic way to acknowledge this relationship and to plant it deep in our spirits, the entire congregation participates in this covenant with the new associates.

Congregation
The crafting of worship is "work that is real." In worship, word and dream, song and deed are woven into the fabric of wonder. We charge you to be weavers.

Associates
This weaving we will do. Speak to us. Tell us of your dreams that we may remind you of them, that we may help you bring them to fruition.

Ministers
We who bear the burden of prayer, we in whom those here gathered place their trust, now place our trust in you. We enlist your courage. We invoke your wisdom. We pledge our cooperation.

Congregation
We call you now into a deeper ministry. We ask you to remember each of us. For each and all are broken. And each and all are beautiful. We charge you to reflect upon both brokenness and beauty as you help to weave the fabric of our community.

Associates
This compassion we will cultivate. This care we will strive to accomplish. We will listen for songs in the night. We will watch what you do and what you refrain from doing, for your deeds and your songs, your dreams and your words are the work of our hearts.

Congregation
Go now, therefore, and be ye the weavers of worth. Speak with us. Dream with us. Sing with us. Strive with us. This trust is a gift freely given.

The impact of the Worship Associates Program has penetrated all the structures, connections, and relationships within the congregation. The program has showed us a new way to be Unitarian Universalists. The next program we developed was the pastoral associates, followed by the education associates, and now we are struggling with the development of the justice associates.

The change in worship in turn changed our congregation. Ownership of the worship experience shifted, as the laity discovered that they are not dependent on the minister to serve up a quality worship experience. More and

more people began to understand that as active participants we all share in the responsibility and the pleasure of
cocreating our shared experience. Worship is a conversation for the entire congregation.

~

*Beverly Sadownick Smrha, Pacific Central District Co-
Executive, has participated in the development of the lay
ministry/associates programs at the First Unitarian Church
of Oakland since 1983. Prior to her work with the PCD,
she served for eight years as Associate to the President for
Communications and Development, at Starr King School for
the Ministry, a theological laboratory of shared ministry.*

Dispatches from a Racially and Culturally Diverse Frontier

Anthony Y. Stringer

No matter how full the river, it still wants to grow.

——AFRICAN PROVERB

Lay ministry has a fundamental role to play in our mission to build intentionally diverse faith communities. These communities will have multiple, sometimes conflicting, theological, liturgical, and spiritual needs. People in these communities will have varying histories that shape their aspirations for power and leadership. A partnership, with professional ministry forming the stable center around which lay ministry orbits, is the best option for growing and sustaining a diverse community of faith.

Lay ministry provides a means of tapping the knowledge, skill, and lore of the various communities that will feed the congregation. It ensures that some portion of the church leadership will share the sensibilities and affirm the aspirations of the differing sets of people making up the congregation. Lay ministry is often a ministry of reconciliation, helping to overcome the barrier of language and the polarity of opposite needs and beliefs, and facilitating the acceptance of a minister who differs in color, culture, gender, or sexual orientation from what some in the congregation would want. Lay ministry allows for greater experimentation, greater creativity, and ultimately greater inclusivity.

Life on the frontier of diversity assuredly will continue to be challenging, frustrating, even infuriating. Attracting people to a diverse community and keeping them are not easy. Confronting the same barriers, arguments, and intransigent attitudes, issue after issue and time after time, drains the spirit. Why do it, especially in that most intimate of all communities, the community of faith and worship? We do it because, like the proverb says, though the river is full, it still wishes to grow.

As so many public institutions abandon diversity these days, it has never been more important for the church to embrace it. I am a charter member and president of Thurman Hamer Ellington (T.H.E.) Church—a church that has made diversity of membership the core of its mission. Our name was chosen to honor the African American theologian Howard Thurman, the civil rights activist Fannie Lou Hamer, and the composer Edward Kennedy "Duke" Ellington.

We are a Unitarian Universalist church, part of a denomination which, in spite of our historical commitment to tolerance and civil rights activism, has never expanded significantly beyond a white urban and suburban base. My church lies at a denominational frontier. The struggles to enact its mission have led me to believe that lay ministry is an essential component in the effort to achieve diversity. The story of our church is a story of lay ministry not quite born.

In 1985, a committee convened in Atlanta to study ways in which Unitarian Universalism could expand into untapped communities. The committee eventually proposed four new churches, one targeting African Americans and one focused on the gay and lesbian community. The proposal was rejected by the existing Atlanta Unitarian Universalist churches, who feared competition and loss of members. The one exception was the proposed African American church. Since few black people had been attracted to the existing churches, no one felt threatened.

No black ministers were available within the denomination, so the proposal for an African American-focused church lingered. Then, in 1988, the Reverend Daniel Aldridge entered the denomination. Already fellowshipped in the United Church of Christ, Aldridge was in the process of becoming a Unitarian Universalist minister. Impressed by Aldridge's energy, commitment, and history of social activism, local leaders arranged a meeting with potential donors. Swayed perhaps by nostalgia for their own involvement with the civil rights movement and by Aldridge's considerable oratory skill, a group of white, liberal Unitarian Universalists enthusiastically embraced the concept of an African American-centered church and signed on as donors. An amount of $35,000 was raised for the new church.

Aldridge's commitments, however, delayed his arrival in Atlanta by eighteen months, adding to the initial two-year delay in enacting the original proposal.

Once Aldridge arrived, nearly all the early work fell to him and not surprisingly, progress was slow. After months of searching largely on his own, Aldridge settled on holding services at a local Holiday Inn. The first black congregants, most entirely new to Unitarian Universalism, began meeting here with white members from the covenanting congregation, who attended services to show their support for the fledgling church. There were often as many as forty to fifty people, mostly white, at these early services.

Despite Aldridge's attempt to welcome all who came, the presence and role of white people in the church remained controversial. The controversy initiated the first flight of members, black and white. Black people left because they felt uncomfortable being a minority in what they thought was to be a black church. White people left because they feared their presence was hindering the church's ability to attract black people. With a second fundraising drive, another $30,000 was raised, again largely from white donors. With ten to fifteen active members, the church moved to afternoon services at a Quaker meetinghouse.

Grant money from the Unitarian Universalist Association helped the church launch a remarkable social outreach program: a choir composed entirely of African percussion instruments. Through appearances in churches and music festivals, the choir became visible, popular, and self-sustaining, but it failed to add more than a handful of new members to the church. Intended to attract black people to the church, T.H.E. choir instead reinforced the church's identity crisis. While it began with a racially mixed membership, the number of black choir members gradually diminished as white members increased.

In 1994, Aldridge accepted the senior minister position at All Souls Church in Washington, DC. Since he personally had shouldered nearly all the activities necessary to sustain the church community, his leaving raised the possibility that the church would have to close its doors. Everyone knew that African American ministers were still scarce in the denomination.

Our next minister was the Reverend Frances West, a capable, experienced, and white Unitarian Universalist minister. Her appointment as interim extension minister intensified the conflicts and anger around mission and identity. Soon, established white members left and potential white members stayed away, no longer sure they were welcome. Some established black members left, too.

In the minds of T.H.E. congregants, the appointment of a white minister to the pulpit was tantamount to being colonized. It seemed to reenact 400 years of oppressive relationships and to throw in the congregants' faces their powerlessness over the destiny of their church. This was neither intended nor foreseen by the UUA, whose focus was on rescuing a church ill prepared to shoulder burdens previously borne by the minister.

The African American community has conflicting expectations of its leadership. Leaders must simultaneously be of, and apart from, the community. They must be peers to whom you can readily relate. But they also must possess some knowledge, skill, expertise, or quality not found in your neighbors. Familiarity guarantees their acceptance, exceptionality their leadership. African American leaders must be, in the truest sense, first among equals.

From these observations it does not necessarily follow, however, that in all instances the church's leaders must be African American. Inevitably, a minister will not look like or share the heritage and sensibilities of everyone in any congregation. In an intentionally diverse congregation, the minister conceivably may look like almost no one. In these instances, the UUA's extension appointment process deserves reexamination. The traditional procedure is that the appointed minister spends several days in the congregation, delivers a sermon, and then leaves to allow the congregation to make up its mind. In other words, the process is designed to win the congregation's confidence. But in intentionally diverse congregations, winning the congregation's acceptance is just as vital as winning its confidence.

Her visit established the Reverend West as a competent and able Unitarian Universalist minister. She had passed the community's test of leadership. The test of acceptance was another matter. The history of race relations in this country being what it is, some congregants never could reach back when West reached out. She eventually was accepted into the hearts of most congregants at T.H.E., but the better part of her ministry was spent gaining this acceptance, and when it came, it was due to familiarity and not professional distance.

The difficulties in forging an inclusive identity came into sharp relief during a sermon from West. In an effort to help the church picture its place within Unitarian Universalism, West drew a timeline illustrating the history of T.H.E. Church. At one end was 1586, when King John Sigismund issued an edict for religious tolerance in Transylvania. At the opposite end of the timeline was the signing of T.H.E. Church's covenant on May 16, 1993. In between were various events in Unitarian Universalist history that were obscure to most of the congregants.

The congregation grew restless. Where were Martin Luther King and Malcolm X? Where were those we chose to honor in the naming of our church? Whose history was this? In fact, whose church was this?

At this point, West held out a piece of chalk and invited the congregation to recreate the timeline, adding the heritage she had missed. After an uncomfortable minute, a young African American male, dressed in cutoffs and the kind of gym shoes that defy lacing, stepped up and claimed the chalk. Turning to the congregation, he offered to add the events we wished to claim as part of our spiritual heritage.

Thirty minutes later, the timeline stretched as far back as Akhnaton's declaration of devotion to one God in the fourteenth century BCE and included events that had taken place on every continent but Australia—events of spiritual significance to people of African ancestry, European ancestry, and Native American ancestry, to feminists, homosexuals, environmentalists, and civil and human rights activists.

In that thirty minutes, this young man had become a partner in the church's ministry. By joining with him, West had allowed the congregation to do what it could only do for itself: define a heritage, if not an identity, that was inclusive of what mattered to the people in this congregation. While it was possible to find an inclusive heritage during the time allotted to one Sunday sermon, the search for a common lexicon is ongoing.

Through this challenging interim extension ministry, West was a model of patience, tolerance, and compassion. She focused on building an organizational foundation that would sustain the church regardless of who was minister. This was perhaps the true beginning of lay ministry at T.H.E. Around this time, a third and final fund drive was held, with a financial goal of $80,000 over three years. The final amount raised fell far short of this goal. A sea change had occurred in the liberal, white, Unitarian Universalist community of Atlanta. Churches that had received far less support questioned this philanthropy. Potential donors said that the well was running dry and would remain so until there was demonstrable membership growth at the African American church.

In 1995 T.H.E. received its third and in many respects its most remarkable minister, the Reverend Dr. Anthony Ephirim-Donkor. A native and village king of Ghana, a graduate of Emory University's Candler School of Theology, and an ordained Methodist minister, Donkor came to T.H.E. Church as a guest speaker and there discovered Unitarian Universalism. Intent upon becoming a fellowshipped Unitarian Universalist minister, Donkor became our next extension minister (in an acting capacity). Now with twenty-two active members and its new black minister, T.H.E. Church established itself in a community meetinghouse in Decatur, Georgia, and opened for Sunday morning services.

Donkor brought a strong, minister-centered leadership style common to African American churches. He brought an unquestioned reverence for the rituals and beliefs of his homeland and the dynamic, emotion-filled homiletic style of the southern black preacher. He brought an explicitly stated commitment to help the church fulfill its mission, which he conceptualized as its becoming a "black" church, which precipitated T.H.E. Church's third identity crisis.

One Sunday, a member read a story to the congregation's children. The story, taken from a Unitarian Universalist children's religious education curriculum, prominently featured a trouble-making black cloud. It didn't go over well. Discussion after service focused on the story rather than the sermon. My suggestion that we all "lighten up"—after all, it was a black cloud and not a black sambo—didn't go over well either.

An even more serious instance of unintended insult occurred when a black churchgoer complained that our percussion choir was not representative of the church because it had too few black faces. A white member of the choir suggested that if the black churchgoer wanted to see more black faces she should bring hers to choir rehearsals.

As hurtful as the dialogue subsequently became between these two well-intentioned members of our community, the incident led to a lovely kind of shuttle diplomacy initiated by an elder black member of the congregation. With gentle insight and humor, this "stateswoman" embarked on a ministry of reconciliation. She explained to the one congregant how hard it can be to find the right words to express something normally as welcome as an invitation, and explaining to the other congregant how for a host of historical and social reasons, a phrase like "bring your black face" is not easy on the ears of an African American when uttered by someone white. As we strive to find words that will bridge the gulfs that separate us, we depend upon those people, like this elder woman, who have learned to talk in many tongues.

A diverse community is not created simply by one group's welcoming another to its way of doing things. No matter how welcoming, the church must embrace not only new people but also new ways of experiencing, worshiping, talking about, and singing the praises of the sacred. The principle is the same whether it is a white congregation welcoming new black members or a black congregation struggling to keep its white members. Diverse churches require diversity in their liturgy. But how are we lifted up spiritually in the midst of this diversity?

Most of us seek, expect, even demand transcendence of self and circumstance when we go to church. African

Americans have poignant historical reasons for seeking this transcendence. A transcendent Sunday experience was often the thin tissue separating a slave from committing murder or suicide or from suffering a less dramatic death of spirit. When the pain is great, the means to transcend must also be great. Hence the character of traditional African American worship—with its music, its pace, its preaching—is loud, up-tempo, swelling to emotional release.

What lifts us up is an individual matter. For some it is the smell of incense or a melodic chant. For others it is the refined harmony of classical music or the intuited truths of Emerson. For one, transcendence may lie in spoken prayer, for another in quiet meditation. Unitarian Universalist churches are known for housing multiple theological perspectives, even when every member is white. Add cultural diversity to the mix, and the burgeoning of perspectives reaches exponential numbers.

Because of this theological diversity, Unitarian Universalist ministers must wear many hats in meeting the needs of their contentious congregations. They have many means of "lifting it up." I admire this in our ministers, and I have compassion for their predicament. It seems to be an impossible job.

But the real task for a minister in a diverse community is less to meet the multiple theological and emotional needs of congregants than to nurture the skills in congregants that will allow them to meet each other's needs. T.H.E. has had three exceptional ministers in its brief history, three people who could not have differed more in their strengths and approaches. Yet not one could meet the needs of all, or even a majority, in this diverse congregation.

The proposal to create our African American-focused church suffered for lack of someone to enact it. District leadership explicitly recognized the contradiction in a group of white Americans, no matter how liberal and well-intentioned, trying to birth a black church. Rather than forge blindly ahead, the district chose to wait for an African American minister to appear and then humbly trusted that he or she would know what to do. This waiting delayed enactment of the proposal, put inordinate responsibility on the shoulders of one person, and kept church-building knowledge and skill away from the fledgling congregation. Before there was a new church, the embrace of new members could have begun and could have extended beyond the minister.

It has been argued that black people can't be racists. According to this argument, it is not prejudice alone that delineates a racist, it is the power to act on that prejudice. Compared to whites, black people do not have the power to enact their prejudices. I find this argument disingenuous. If not racist, what do we call an attitude that allows for no one but an African American as minister of T.H.E. Church? If not racist, what do we call a proposal to exclude all but black members of the congregation from board offices? If not racist, what do we make of the description of T.H.E. as a black church? I can think of no other word to describe a church that calls itself white, elects only whites to board positions, and will accept only a white minister. How can the word racist apply in one instance and not the other?

Still, it can be legitimately argued that an intentionally black church is needed in a denomination that has so few black people. It can be argued that our minority status makes legitimate our aspirations to power in our church board. On grounds of practicality alone, we can justify our insistence upon a black minister. If our mission is to attract black people—and few black people will come to a church pastored by a white person—then we must have a black minister to enact our mission.

These are the murky waters we wade in at T.H.E. So how do we navigate? Principle dictates one thing, practicality another. Our desire to be fair to all people seeking a spiritual home sets us on one course, and our aspirations as a long oppressed minority pull us to another. If we follow principle only, we lose sight of the people involved. If we yield to seemingly legitimate desires, we risk compromising our values. Yet, it is in compromise that a way may be found. Compromise lies in the blending and resolution of extremes, in the rejection of either/or assertions.

A church like T.H.E. does not have to choose between white and black ministry; it can have both. Indeed it should demand both, all three, or as many as are needed. Diverse congregants require diverse ministries. Lay ministry offers this option, not as a replacement of professional ministry, but as a supplement to it. Offering the possibility of lay

ministry recognizes the murkiness of the waters we sometimes wade in and acknowledges that in many arguments
there is truth on both sides.

Strong lay ministry would have helped T.H.E. stay on a
stable course instead of veering in many directions in its
short lifetime. It has been a church focused on political
and social justice, a church focused on ending violence
against women, a church focused on artistic expression,
and a church seeking inspiration in the rituals of Africa.
Through much of its history, the church has been plagued
by a lack of depth in its membership. Few members were
Unitarian Universalists before they stumbled upon T.H.E.
The demographics of Unitarian Universalism being what
they are, the experienced Unitarian Universalist members
have tended to be white. Hence, when the church has
seemed to veer too far in one direction or another, the call
back to the center often has been issued by white
congregants. This adds a racial dimension to every discussion of the church's direction and mission.

The same dynamic happens in discussions of theology.
Because of the theological diversity of our congregations,
every Unitarian Universalist church deals with issues of
proportion and balance. Though sometimes contentious,
the discussions around these issues are essentially healthy.
Yet they take on an entirely different quality in churches
like T.H.E., where the humanists, atheists, deists, and ag-
nostics are white and their disputants are not. The subtle
geometry of theological debate is never as easy to grasp as
the grosser calculus of race.

Today T.H.E. Church remains a work in progress. Though membership has never climbed much beyond twenty, it has managed to support most of its operations and expenses from member contributions. UUA funds have been used primarily to support ministry. Though the smallest and poorest of the Atlanta Unitarian Universalist churches, T.H.E. has given birth to a unique social outreach project in the form of its percussion choir—the choir is a resource and publicity vehicle for the entire district. Through its struggles to define itself and to meld contentiously different people into a community of faith, T.H.E. has been a frontier of diversity.

Diverse congregations require intentionally diverse ministries and strong centers. As T.H.E. has veered, so have its ministers. Sometimes they have led and other times they have followed the congregation in its meanderings. Our ministers have served us best when they have provided a strong Unitarian Universalist center, a center that anchors without confining, stabilizes without suppressing, and provides ground to return to when we've flown too far. The task of the UUA is less to match ministers to congregations than to provide centers for congregations. In churches like T.H.E., when lay ministries that resonate to the needs of the diverse congregants are in partnership with a Unitarian Universalist center, the color of that center matters less than its stability.

Our pull toward diversity is a lively, loving thing. Despite our capacity for prejudice and polarization, we lust for community. Though we may fear the stranger, we are also attracted. Our comfort in the familiar does not diminish our intrigue with the mysterious. While the known resassures us, growth lies in encountering the unknown. Like the river, we want to grow.

~

Anthony Stringer is a charter member of the Thurman Hamer Ellington Church, an intentionally diverse Unitarian Universalist congregation in Decatur, Georgia. Tony is president of the board and chairs the Lay Ministry Committee at his church. He is also cofounder of the Thurman Hamer Ellington percussion choir and is a trustee of The Mountain, the Unitarian Universalist camp and conference center in Highlands, North Carolina.

The Youth Conference Community

Rob Cavenaugh

When I was in the ninth grade in 1990, I was a varsity football player, wrestler, and cocaptain of the track team. I was voted Student of the Month and "Biggest Flirt." Like most of my classmates, I began that year as a homophobic, sexist, and racist individual.

I've grown up Unitarian Universalist. Both my parents are die-hard, church-going, coffee-making, children-watching, committee-serving Unitarian Universalists. They've been a positive influence I can't overestimate. Nevertheless, society planted seeds of prejudice in me. Though I've spent the last five years trying to weed out my biases, I probably will still be weeding fifty years from now.

I actually did something important in ninth grade. I joined the youth group at the Unitarian Church of Harrisburg, Pennsylvania. It was there, one Sunday morning, that I decided to tell a joke. I probably wasn't getting the attention I wanted, and what better way to get attention?

Afterward, I was shocked when nearly everyone remained silent. I got attention, but not the kind I wanted. Back then I hadn't even heard of homophobia, and sharing homophobic jokes wasn't unusual for me. When one of my older friends asked, "Why do you think that's funny?" I had no reply. That was one of the most important questions anyone ever asked me. I thought of my repertoire of jokes. Whether it was homophobia, racism, or sexism, I had humor for all of it.

Pretty soon I figured out that arbitrarily insulting certain groups was indeed a problem. The catalyst for this was my exposure to other Unitarian Universalist youth at district youth conferences—in the Joseph Priestley District we simply called them "cons." I'd heard cons were really cool, but I was unsure of what to expect—I'd never yet met a Unitarian Universalist youth who wasn't from my own church. On the way to the conference, along with other first-timers, I was nervous. I was glad the older youth in the group were there, even though they were mercilessly educating me on Unitarian Universalist values and beliefs. As a friend and I entered the church lobby, our anxiety was peaking. The sight of a huge pile of personal belongings and the registration table relaxed us a bit. Being asked by the girl running through the lobby if we were ticklish had the opposite effect. We said "no."

After registering and adding our stuff to the pile, we took a look around. Everywhere people were talking, hugging, laughing, and looking generally glad to see each other. Some were even happy to see us, though they'd never seen us before. Later on that evening, after a big meeting to explain rules and logistics, we divided into small groups and herded off to meeting places. We did introductions, learned that we were responsible for either preparing or cleaning up after a meal, heard a little about the conference theme and workshops, and played some games. It took me a while that weekend to get used to everything, but by the time Sunday morning came I knew I was hooked.

Conferences quickly became a vital part of my life. For four or five weekends each year of high school, I escaped into the open, accepting, loving, trusting, and affectionate atmosphere of the conference community. In ninth grade I found a home in Young Religious Unitarian Universalists (YRUU), and I also found I had much to learn about myself. As I attended workshops and worship, and as I played games and spent hours talking with friends, I was seeking out my identity. For the first time I could call myself a Unitarian Universalist with some idea of what that meant. Consciously and unconsciously, I started fighting sexism, racism, and homophobia—in myself and in general.

YRUU is lay ministry. As a spiritual community, youth search for their individual beliefs and help others do the same. Effective advisors provide the wisdom of experience without shaping beliefs or stifling curiosity; no ministers lead the spiritual journeys of YRUU members. Everyone is invited to take an active role in worship, as participants and as leaders. The word *service* is rarely associated with youth worship, except when youth are asked to participate on Sunday mornings. For me, worship and lay ministry are not services, they are actions. And they are to be undertaken equally by all.

My experience with youth lay ministry informs my outlook as a young adult. The current age range for young adults in the Unitarian Universalist Association is eighteen to thirty-five, allowing for some overlap between youth and young adult stages. Some young adults enter college immediately, some enter the job market, others take time off from both. All have the pressures of school, jobs, or careers hanging over them. These new challenges lead to a lot of soul-searching, though the pressure and other circumstances can make self-exploration very difficult. Young adults are making choices about who they are and what they want out of life.

YRUU helped me find my identity before these troubled times set in. Many people I know, myself included, have fallen into the trap of trying first to find the part of their identity that is separate and removed from society, and then trying to relate who they are to the world around them. Like it or not, the forces of society are powerful and unavoidable. We all are shaped by them and must deal with them; including the forces of gender, race, and sexuality.

Ask yourself: What position does your gender have in society? Does your skin color entitle you to privilege or subject you to persecution? Do you easily fit into the societal categories of man and woman, or are you labeled as an outsider?

I am a straight, white male, and society accords me

power and privilege. I realize that throughout history many have used such a position for self-advancement, and continue to do so today. This is the mold that made me. Do I like it? No. But if I did not discover and accept these things about my identity, my ability to create change would be severely restricted.

As it is, despite my good intentions, my insight and abilities are limited—I cannot truly understand what it is like to be gay, or a person of color, or a female, or a transgendered person.

With Unitarian Universalism as a driving force, however, I have made a firm commitment to righting some of the wrongs that have been perpetrated by people with power and privilege. I identify and draw inspiration from a feeling of collective good—the notion that we humans are capable of existing in harmony with each other and with the Earth. This conviction, developed through my experiences in YRUU, fuels my commitment to social justice.

In youth circles, this feeling is generally known as "the conference community." Everyone is expected to respect the community and not to do things that disrupt it. Illegal drug use does not benefit the community. Exploring sexuality and sexual identity through conversation benefits individuals and promotes a sense of trust in the community. Sexual activity, on the other hand, benefits only those involved and fractures the conference community. Everyone's commitment to the conference community ensures the levels of trust and acceptance that make self-growth possible. I have never found another community in which safety and love were valued as much by so many.

YRUU provides a great community for exploring one's identity, identifying with Unitarian Universalism, and being inspired to social justice. YRUU is effective because it is essentially a lay ministry. A lot of things happened between the time I entered YRUU in ninth grade and when I left in 1996. I graduated from high school, went to college, moved seven times, and held seven different jobs. Did YRUU and my experience with lay ministry help shape those years? You better believe it!

Young adults need to experience this sort of community. Young adults who experienced YRUU probably seek a more spiritual community than exists in our congregations on Sunday mornings. Those just finding Unitarian Universalism may feel similarly. To me, a spiritual community is a group of people who are sharing a spiritual experience together. As an association that emphasizes a free and responsible search for truth and meaning, we know that each individual's spiritual experience will be different. Without a significant amount of sharing during worship, how can a congregation grow spiritually? If it is better to give than to receive, why are so many people at worship sitting and receiving? It is true that sermons help us grow as individuals, at least emotionally or intellectually, if not spiritually. Sunday services do this very well. But we as an association need to grow as a spiritual community, together. We need lay ministry, all day, every day. Like faith, lay ministry should not be confined to certain places, people, or times. It should be lived, eaten, breathed, walked, and talked.

In many large cities and some large congregations, young adult groups exist as either a supplement or an alternative to the regular service. Some groups are mostly social, but most have a deliberate spiritual mission. It's good that we have young adult groups because it means there are young adults interested in Unitarian Universalism. But the existence of young adult groups also indicates that Sunday services are not satisfying to our age group. Though young adult groups are often able to provide the necessary extra interaction, they require a great deal of time and energy to maintain. I am concerned that young adult groups will come and go in the short run and the problem of unsatisfying services will remain.

Young adults benefit enormously when lay ministry becomes an inherent component of our faith. I benefited from YRUU, and I wish many others could have shared my experience. I'm not advocating the creation of a young adult YRUU. I am advocating the creation of meaningful communities where young adults can explore, develop, and share their beliefs. With the prominence of conservative religious movements, many liberal young adults show little interest in religion. If I can show my friends and people I meet that there's such a thing as liberal religion, perhaps more young adults will take an interest in their own beliefs and maybe in Unitarian Universalism as well.

In my second semester at college, I was selected by the YRUU steering committee to fill an unexpected vacancy as a programs specialist in the Youth Office at the UUA's offices in Boston. Working as a YRUU programs specialist is more office work than other forms of lay ministry, but like previous experiences, it increased my desire to become more involved in church activities. I am committed to bringing more lay ministry to Unitarian Universalism, especially now as a member of the Young Adult Ministries Advisory and Outreach Task Force. The Task Force assists and advises the young adult ministries coordinator and addresses the needs of young adult Unitarian Universalists.

Our faith continues to thrive despite the conspicuous absence of young adults, especially eighteen- to twenty-five-year-olds. Think of the unrealized potential represented by those missing individuals. And lay ministry is part of Unitarian Universalism, but we have the potential for so much more. By placing more emphasis on lay ministry, and by creating better environments for worship and spiritual growth in our congregations and on our campuses, we can accomplish so much.

Should we bother to work for these goals? When I compare who I am today with the homophobic, racist, and sexist ninth grader I was in 1990, I know the answer is "yes."

∼

Rob Cavenaugh has been active in Unitarian Universalism since age 17, when he was first elected to the Joseph Priestley District Youth Steering Committee. He currently resides in Washington, DC, where he is very involved in both young adult and campus ministry and social justice organizing.

The Ministry of Lay Leadership

Linda Lane-Hamilton

Starting a church is exhilarating and exhausting. It's a step into space from the safety of the ship. You wonder: Where will this step take us? How will we shape the journey?

New churches start in many ways. A minister or lay leader has a vision. Extension or growth committees conduct demographic studies. Larger churches spin off new groups or "covenant" to support new congregations. And occasionally a group of members stomp off, angry at the "mother church," and set up one on their own.

In our case, we began as a grassroots start. In 1988 the Williamsburg, Virginia, area had been without a Unitarian Universalist congregation for several years after a small fellowship here had dwindled and folded. I'd been active in that fellowship for some time and had participated in its disintegration. Looking back, I see we were too small to offer formal worship, too small to provide buffers when arguments arose, and too divided in our purpose.

After we broke up, I joined a fellowship twenty-five

miles down the road, out of town, where I met my husband and we eventually married. We built leadership skills in that group, my husband as worship chair and moderator and both of us as youth advisors. But the fellowship was out of town, so we didn't see church friends at the grocery store or on the job, and we did not have a social action link to Williamsburg, where we lived. Furthermore, this fellowship was uncertain about the role of professional ministry and worship, both of which we valued.

During my last years there, I felt my needs shifting. I wanted a church that was sophisticated and deeply religious. I wanted a minister, a choir, and meditation. I wanted church to start on time, to have answers as well as questions, and to be serious about itself. And I wanted a place in my own town where we could celebrate birth, marriage, and death with other Unitarian Universalists.

Our district executive came to visit at just the right time. The night before his visit, I spent a restless night dreaming about starting a church, the questions we could ask, the phone calls to make, people to call. The next morning, my husband and I cornered the district executive right after the service: "Williamsburg is ready, we want to start a church. What do we do?" "I will send you materials," he said. "Gather the people," he said. His words echoed, and still do. Gather the people into the dream, into the community, into worship, and into the reality of the church.

That summer we gathered people phone call by phone call. Each call was carefully made to a Unitarian Universalist who might share our vision of a religious home for us and our children. We called local Unitarian Universalists who had knowledge and experience but who were unchurched or were driving long distances to another congregation. One man, a physics professor who would later become a gifted leader, spoke of a delightful irony: twenty years earlier he had begun the Williamsburg fellowship with his first family of two young children. Now he would begin a second congregation with his second family, two daughters who would now grow up Unitarian Universalist. Another phone call went to a woman who had been born a Unitarian Universalist forty years earlier, and whose eventual membership would honor her own Unitarian Universalist father.

We gathered people we thought shared our vision. We knew some Unitarian Universalists who would be less comfortable than we were with ministry, meditation, prayer, and spirituality. We believed this church could be a welcoming place for them someday, but not yet.

We openly recruited unchurched friends. If we thought they shared our values, we approached them. Our first gathering was a potluck. We had no program, no opening or closing words. "Is this all?" one person asked. "Are we doing anything else tonight?" "No," we said. But these questions reminded us that we were more than a potluck, and more than coffee, and that something was missing.

Our district executive said, "Gather the people again when I visit Williamsburg over Labor Day." And so ten of us circled up in our living room. "Why are you here?" he asked, a question we continue to ask newcomers today. That night we spoke of unspoken needs, the dream, the church.

The district executive gave simple, practical advice. *Take it slow. Don't start worship too soon. Don't write bylaws or do church business too soon. First build a community that can agree on the shape of the church. Get to know one another religiously.* He asked us to take hands, a move so simple yet so unfamiliar that someone expressed discomfort. But we were connected, drawn together in purpose.

From this point on, we added the missing dimension from our first potluck: opening words, a reading, a closing circle—something to remind us that we were more than a potluck, more than coffee hour—we were an emerging religious community. We were fortunate to have members who were spiritual leaders: my husband, who feels at home with metaphor, and the physics professor, a gifted writer whose words sing. They offered us language that invited introspection, they used words to inspire and guide. They, along with others, ministered to us and reminded us of the holy in our midst.

We began building community. We invited people we thought might be interested to monthly Friday night gatherings. These meetings were small and spiritual. We worshiped together briefly—a reading, music, wise words from the thoughtful among us. We introduced occasional business items, but personal, social, and spiritual matters dominated. We shaped a carefully structured discussion for each gathering, with leaders who broke us into small groups and then pulled us back together to share information.

Our topics seemed simple: What are our personal religious histories? What meaningful religious and worship experiences have we had? How has ministry made a difference in our lives? How has religious education been meaningful to us?

These subjects provided the crucial framework for our future church. As we talked, we deepened our understanding, and miraculously we found harmony among ourselves. We valued worship and professional ministry. We would be a religious community with intellectually challenging and spiritually focused programs. We wanted music and art and light-filled space to worship in. We wanted religious education for our children and for us.

We also benefited from our varied experiences with other Unitarian Universalist congregations—large and small, formal churches and informal fellowships. We knew from experience that some congregations disagree about ministry, the use of religious language, social action programs, and the role of humanism, paganism, Christianity, and other belief systems. We recognized the importance of community building to help us define who we would become in the midst of so many options.

We did not yet know that we were lay ministers. We saw ourselves as eager volunteers, shaping a bit of local Unitarian Universalist history. But we considered ministry as other than ourselves, ministers as those men and women who earn professional degrees and know how to do special things. We counted on the advice and connections of others who had more experience. Though we had the vision, we could not always see the path.

We leaned on the ministry of our district executive, a

professional representative of the church and himself a layperson. He kept us from feeling isolated, suggested a pace for our community building, provided us with resources and connections to others who had started new congregations, and returned every telephone call. It was a passing of the baton, in a sense—his knowledge was passed on to a small group, still wandering and uncertain, and this small group later passed that knowledge on to others. Close ties with him during those years helped us do things the right way.

He connected us with two groups we came to call our "sister churches." These groups had formed a year before we did, and their lay members provided valuable ministry to us. An organizer of the Piedmont church near Charlotte, North Carolina, gave us hope that our community building would work. A lay leader of the Westside (Knoxville) group described their meeting space in a public school, leading us eventually to rent a spacious, lofty cafeteria in our newest elementary school. They told us of their commitment to two- or three-year terms as leaders to provide continuity to their young congregations. Lay leaders from both groups answered our questions: How long before you had a public meeting? When did you begin worship services? How did you choose leaders? Their responses helped us grow the idea that we could become a congregation of Unitarian Universalists some day.

Our district executive provided advisors, called New Congregation Organizers (NCOs). For one year, our first NCO drove 120 miles round trip to facilitate discussions and introduce us to the video series on Unitarian Universalism. She was followed by another appointed lay volunteer, an experienced church leader who today is employed by the Unitarian Universalist Association. Each NCO brought a start-up grant of $1,000 from Unitarian Universalist headquarters. In addition to paying the expenses of our organizers, the money eventually was used to purchase a chalice, Unitarian Universalist handbooks, and religious education materials.

We continued to seek others who could minister to us. One woman, highly recommended as a group facilitator, taught the adult religious education course "Building Your Own Theology." She drove from central North Carolina to Williamsburg three weekends to lead the course, giving her time and talents for free. Over a dozen emerging Unitarian Universalists gathered in our living room to discuss their own religious backgrounds and beliefs.

We found an historian from the Norfolk church who drove to Williamsburg to teach us Unitarian Universalist history. His session was particularly meaningful, since it linked our Unitarian Universalist group to Williamsburg's early history. We learned that many English Unitarians had emigrated to the American colonies—primarily Boston, Philadelphia, and Williamsburg—in search of religious freedom. In fact, the College of William and Mary had been a center of Unitarian thought from the 1740s through the Revolution. We learned that anti-Unitarian attitudes here forced several professors to remain "closet" Unitarians, including one who was tried in the Bruton Parish Episcopal Church tower. We marveled that William and Mary had actually been known as a "hotbed of heresy and Unitarian thought."

The contributions of these volunteers broadened our connection to the denomination and helped us build our understanding of Unitarian Universalism. They also helped us realize that one day we could help others as they formed new congregations. Our journey in Williamsburg was linking us with the larger faith community.

Eventually, we knew that our leadership needed to take a more institutional shape. On the advice of our district executive, we decided to hold our first public meeting— to announce our presence to the larger community and, again, to gather the people. But going public meant we had to get organized. We now needed a steering committee to make decisions. We volunteered for our parts—secretary, treasurer, cochairs of Sunday services, and myself as reluctant chair who had kept waiting for a leader to surface. We had important decisions to make, keeping in mind that we were a religious community and that we were building community with each decision that established precedent and tradition. We wanted to make the best decisions for a church that had yet to take physical shape.

Beyond our specific tasks, we had a larger function. We had to minister to one another, to keep the vision clear: What did we want from our church? How could we make our church excellent rather than slipshod? How could we be sure of success?

One way was our newsletter. Published almost from the

beginning, *The Williamsburg UU Newsletter* told our emerging story with each issue. Later, when we held formal worship services, the newsletter editor included sermon passages and texts of memorable readings. In each newsletter, the latest additions to our mailing list revealed the growth that was unfolding. More important, we reported the results of each monthly meeting, using participants' actual words to show both the diversity and the common elements in our discussions. By reading these reports, our readers could decide whether they, too, fit in the community they saw developing. Sometimes they didn't, and several long-time members of the original Williamsburg fellowship did not remain involved with our new group.

We ministered to one another during our Friday night community-building sessions. We made our past religious struggles public. We shared our stories. And when we became discouraged because only eight people showed up, our mentor reminded us that we were growing gradually and we should not worry about numbers. We also ministered to one another in special ways—such as the evening we set aside for men to respond to a tape by Robert Bly. And we continued to be ministered to in worship, traveling to Norfolk and Richmond for occasional Sunday services.

As lay ministers, we fought discouragement. Each criticism, each loss of member could be taken personally, a portent for disaster. We had to deal with the few naysayers at fragile and crucial moments while continuing to hold onto our vision, the dream of worshiping together as a

Unitarian Universalist congregation. Some doubters feared that it would not work, that there would be too few people. Others had a different vision, preferring fellowships that featured discussion and debate, more narrowly drawn than our new group. Some wanted proof that the group would make it before committing to any work.

Sometimes the work seemed insurmountable. We all had other things to do—teach physics or Portuguese or law at William and Mary, teach French or English at the local high school, work in the computer center, paint, practice therapy, raise young children. Many of us worked full-time at demanding jobs and then spent as many as thirty hours some weeks on the hard labor of bearing a church. Now we look back and wonder how we did it.

Our first public meeting was planned for April 10, 1988. We invited our district executive to lead the service. We arranged for child care and hospitality. We bought advertising in Williamsburg's twice-weekly newspaper (which the community reads almost word-for-word), and we found an amazingly friendly religion editor who eventually put our chalice next to the cross and Star of David on the newspaper's religion page.

The night before our public meeting, we didn't sleep. The next morning, early, we called one another—what if no one comes? The most we had had at a small group session was twenty-five: could we get more? Eighty people attended the service! When they walked in the door, they said, "I've been a Unitarian Universalist all my life." They said, "I've been looking for a church like this." They said,

"Why didn't you tell us sooner? I could have helped." We had so many children we had to recruit babysitters on the spot. That first public meeting was an energizing event for everyone. It sealed our vision to begin regular services twice a month the coming September. Now we would become a church.

We began to reach out from our inner circle. No longer a small family, we expanded to include and welcome the next wave. Our ministry was becoming complex: education for our children, worship for the congregation as a whole. We knew we must minister to social needs, connecting strangers. And yet we must continue to minister to one another.

Sunday services became a priority. Our worship co-chairs wrote a guiding philosophy that emphasized standards for quality and spirituality, specifying that even lectures and performances have a spiritual component ("such as personal morality, social responsibility, religious implications, emotional appeal, relationship between the individual and the community"). To provide variety but show a strong commitment to professional ministry, half the services that first year were led by visiting ministers from as far away as Winston-Salem, North Carolina.

Though the worship services went well, behind the scenes we were exhausted. Even though our ministry had spread, some of us still were doing too much. I chaired religious education, taught the large high school youth group, and headed the steering committee. We kept in mind our commitment to remain as leaders for two to three years and looked longingly toward the end. We knew it would come soon, once we chartered, conducted our first canvass drive, and set up our first board.

We continued being ministered to, but in more structured, institutional ways. Our finance committee attended the district church management seminar. We entered the UUA's New Congregation Ministry program, on the advice of our district executive and the strong recommendation of the steering committee. From a district chalice lighter grant, we received almost $4,000 toward ministerial expenses for our first year of ministry.

We set up new lay ministries, such as a caring committee and a choir—informal but organized enough to sing at our first Christmas service. Fifteen newcomers showed up for our first "New UU" orientation class.

We planned our Charter service for a weekend in February 1989, complete with a dinner social and a lavish reception. We surprised ourselves by wanting to sign the membership book as charter members during the service rather than as a private event afterward. We were used to being religious together, to speaking our commitments out loud, and we were not shy about making a public commitment to our new church.

February 5, 1989, we awoke to a treacherous ice storm, a rarity in Virginia. Phone calls came in from Richmond and sites west: the roads were so bad that guests would be unable to attend their own churches, let alone ours. Our older and frailer friends, trapped by the ice, called and asked to sign the membership book later, when they were able to leave their houses. We promised to leave the book open for them. Those of us too committed to back down chipped and melted ice so we could open our car doors.

We wondered whether anyone would come. But the auditorium was full. And when we asked those wishing to become charter members to rise, almost everyone did. The lines for signing were so long that the volunteer pianist ran out of music. Eighty-nine people signed the book, joined by ten others later that week.

Almost two years had passed since that first conversation with our district executive. In the months that followed the Charter service, we completed bylaws, ran our first canvass, affirmed the appointment of a New Congregation Minister, and began weekly worship and religious education.

Now our ministry goes beyond our local church. We have told our story many times to new congregations. Seven years later, I see that we have turned our dream into a reality. In 1996 the Williamsburg Unitarian Universalists moved into their $750,000 building, described as the "only cathedral in Williamsburg" because of its design. We called our first minister and signed a record sixty-six new members. In the fall of 1996 we began our second capital campaign to purchase the property and house next door to our new church.

We've come a long way, but I still remember the simple question we asked our district executive in 1988: "What do we do to start a church?" And his wonderful answer: "Gather the people."

~

Linda Lane-Hamilton has been a Unitarian Universalist since 1974. She helped organize the Williamsburg Unitarian Universalist Church and served in a variety of leadership roles there. She teaches English, speech, and journalism at the area high school and advises the school newspaper.

Power in Our Congregations

Constance LaFerriere

As I travel around to congregations in my position as district executive, I am struck by the fascination with and the denial of the issue of power, especially as it relates to the dynamics of leadership. Some people and congregations do not rightfully claim the power that they have and so do not accomplish all that they could. Other people use their power to further their own ends and thus subvert the purposes of the congregation. When people enjoy having power, they are suspect, because power must be handled with care. The use or abuse of power has the capacity to make or break our congregations.

What are some of the sources of power in our churches? A person might have power because she or he has an assigned role, such as minister or board president, or credentials, such as education or work experience that gives the person status and respect. Power also derives simply from having a close relationship with such a person. Charisma, knowledge of the workings of the congregation, and resources, such as money, all can give an individual power. A form of power that spills over from society at large to congregations is being a member of a dominant group (Caucasian, physically able, heterosexual, etc.). Finally, simply being in relationships with people gives us power because then we are in a position to influence them.

Any of these sources of power can be used constructively and appropriately, or destructively and inappropriately. When power is used appropriately, those who have it take responsibility to use it to further the aims of the group involved. The power is used to initiate dialogue, to bring people with different ideas and skills together to address the group's purposes and needs and to carry out the work of the church; to create loving, joyous, and exciting religious congregations; and to send out the group's message into the larger community.

People are using power inappropriately when they use it to satisfy their own ego, to push their own agenda without regard for the needs and desires of the group, to subvert the group's mission and purpose, or to manipulate others for their own ends.

When power is misused, several things can happen: (1) Those who feel powerless or "run over" disengage from, and no longer participate in, the church; (2) those who feel less powerful challenge the more powerful, creating an adversarial relationship; or (3) those who feel less powerful gather others to create their own power bloc which will overcome the person(s) in power.

In analyzing what is healthy or dysfunctional in a congregation, I believe we must look to these sources of power and how they are being used. To deny the power inherent in these situations invites chaos or stagnation.

In small congregations, especially, we know that there is usually a "matriarch" or "patriarch" (or both). These leaders can inspire and energize others to form a group that together helps to meet some of the needs of the community—for example, holding worship services, forming study groups, doing social justice work, or providing religious education. When the group continually relies on these patriarchal or matriarchal leaders, however, and the leaders have difficulty sharing their roles ("but no one else will do it!"), the group will usually stay small, if not eventually dry up. Because malice is not involved, but more likely benign paternalism (or maternalism), these leaders often do not see or acknowledge their power. Others in the group accept and reinforce these roles. The longer this lack of awareness continues, the harder it is to break out of this mold.

A generation ago there were clear gender role power differences in our churches (which, of course, reflected the larger society). Almost all ministers (usually the most powerful role in a church) were men, as were the board presidents and treasurers. Women raised the money with activities such as bake sales, and they did the "scut" work as well as teach religious education classes. Much, although not all, of this has changed. We have many women ministers (although most senior ministers—the best paid in our largest churches—are men). Board presidents and finance chairs are often women and do have power, yet religious education, which has traditionally been short-changed in budget and space needs, usually have as their directors less well-paid or well-educated women.

The power struggles in larger churches between the "old" congregants (often humanists or intellectuals) and the new (often younger baby boomers looking for spirituality) seem prevalent in many of our congregations. At a leadership school, a "fish bowl" of each group—in which the group gathers in a circle and discusses how they feel, while the other group simply listens in a circle around the outside—revealed that members of *each* group felt powerless, unappreciated, and undervalued. Congregations that are recognizing and intentionally addressing this power struggle seem able to avoid the "we/they" divisions that can result. When the leadership is consistently sending messages to both groups indicating their value to the institution and showing appreciation for their "differing gifts," the power of each is enhanced. The fear of acknowledging these different power imbalances often leaves our churches with an undercurrent of struggle that saps their energy and prevents their being able to come together in mutual trust and respect. Some seem intent on "being right" rather than having a relationship.

One extreme in the abuse of power is the person to whom we give unlimited power. I think of a small congregation where the president was also the highest pledger. He gave one-third of the church's budget. When the part-time minister behaved in a way the president didn't like, he decided to withhold his pledge and leave the congregation. Because the congregation had relied so heavily on the president's financial contribution, they felt they had no choice but to dismiss the minister. It was many years before they recovered from this disastrous situation.

Another extreme is the power exerted by someone who feels (or acts) abused. I think of the man who was a long-term member of the church, yet had engaged in some questionable practices in handling money entrusted to him. When the board and minister decided to institute some financial checks and balances, he objected. The board then decided that the man would not have access to the church's money in the future. The man was highly incensed, and he gathered others to support him and object to "how he was treated." A great deal of time and energy was expended in trying to appease this man and particularly his supporters, who felt he had been treated unfairly.

This power of a "victim" (one who perceives himself or herself this way) to draw their "rescuers" into their camps, against the "persecutors," is a frequent phenomenon in our congregations. We must analyze the dynamics of problem situations to be sure we are not reinforcing these destructive roles. While we want to protect individual rights, we need to focus more clearly on the needs of the community if we are to preserve the institution so it can effectively further all our aims.

Another aspect of power is seen in the concept of "shared ministry." Traditionally, "the minister" was seen as the only one doing ministry; laypeople were there to support the minister and provide the resources to help him (usually a man) function. In some of our larger churches especially, people still hold on to this concept. The more recent concept of "shared ministry" adopts the philosophy that the professional minister and the laity collaborate to provide the ministry of the congregation. By acknowledging the abilities of church members, and naming this lay contribution as ministry, the power inherent in ministry is diffused. This can be helpful if the respective roles are clearly defined; if it is used to denigrate the gifts, training, and commitment of the professional minister, it can be damaging.

A serious misuse of power, although not as frequent as those mentioned above, is sexual misconduct on the part of a minister, or others in a position of trust, with those more vulnerable than themselves. Sexual misconduct occurs across a broad spectrum, from sexual harassment, unwanted touching, or personal remarks, to having a sexual relationship with a congregant. Sexuality is part of our humanity; in addition, Unitarian Universalism historically has defined itself as "liberal" and therefore often is loath to put constraints on our clergy or youth advisors for fear of being accused of puritanism. What is often described, however, as consensual sex between the parties, or at least collusion, is actually an abuse of power on the part of the minister or advisor. This is why the code of ethics of the Unitarian Universalist Ministers Association clearly spells out these issues and makes it clear that they are a breach of professional ethics and trust.

Many of us have difficulty acknowledging the power of the minister who nearly always has more influence and more charisma, and thus more power, than the victim. One problem in acknowledging this differential is our un-willingness to recognize the vulnerability of the women who come to a church seeking safety and a place to be vulnerable.

This loss of trust in our clergy (or others whom the church has named in positions of authority) can have far-reaching consequences. Congregations that have had to dismiss a minister for sexual misconduct have a hard time regrouping. Younger women, especially, are apt to leave a church where they do not feel safe and where sexuality is used by the minister or people in positions of authority as a form of misplaced power.

At a time when we want to attract young families to our congregations, this breach of trust can have serious consequences. Unless they are particularly needy or vul-nerable, young women today are often less willing to over-look or condone unwanted sexual advances or harassment. If a church is unwilling to address these issues, it can leave itself open to the risk of a lawsuit in addition to the loss of potential valuable members.

It is easier to understand the vulnerability of children. Likewise, when a youth consultant sees him- or herself as one of the youth, there is the potential for abuse of trust. In the *UUA Youth Advisor's Handbook* by Shell Tain, this issue is addressed to youth advisors. It is useful as well for those working with adults. Youth advisors are cautioned to recognize the power inherent in being older, more experienced, more knowledgeable, and more financially secure. They need to learn the concepts of "power over," "power with," and "power within" and recognize the positive uses and abuses of each. Youth advisors can use these concepts to teach youth to understand and use power appropriately—for example, how to move from a one-down position as a child to that of having power with those who are older. The handbook also reminds advisors that the concept of "power within" reflects our Unitarian Universalist value of "the inherent worth and dignity" of every individual and that "power within" is expressed in their own ideas, opinions, feelings, and decision making.

An exercise on power in a congregation is useful, particularly for the lay leadership. Ask participants to place themselves in the room according to how much power they feel they have in the congregation: those closest to the center of the room feel they have the most power, those closest to the walls the least. Then ask them first to describe how it *felt* to place themselves in this way, then to comment on why they chose this location. This process can lead to a valuable discussion and some new awareness of the dynamics of the leadership group.

I believe that we have much greater power than we acknowledge or use. If we can put aside our fear of discussing these issues, we can rejoice in the real power that we have *with* each other, rather than use power *over* one another. When we come together in common accord, we can help change society as we did in the civil rights era and as we do now with our stand on gay rights. We create inspiring services and new ways of dealing with problems that we share at General Assembly. Our congregations in many cases provide sources of inspiration and comfort, of celebration and community which have changed people's lives. We do have power and we can use it to bring our influence to a larger segment of society. Let us own that power!

~

Constance LaFerriere is the District Executive of the Pacific Southwest District, now in her eighth year. Formerly a professor and counselor in a community college, she also volunteered in Unitarian Universalist churches and other organizations for many years while raising five children and living in many parts of this country and around the world.

The $^\$$M$^\$$ Word

Jeri Moulder

My life took a big turn in 1982 when we moved from California to New Orleans and joined the First Unitarian Universalist Church there. Fourteen years later my resume would include such activities as chair of the yearly canvass, member of the church finance committee, chair of a capital campaign, and member of the finance committee for The Mountain (the camp and conference center), culminating with a job as a fundraising consultant for the Unitarian Universalist Association. What happened? How did my feelings about the church and money change from misery to ministry?

Like many in my generation, I grew up in a home where money was rarely mentioned and dealing with my weekly allowance of twenty-five cents was my only contact with finances. I vaguely knew when my daddy's business was losing money. My mother was a young woman during the depression and the only working member in a family of six. She never lost that depression mentality and was a frequenter of the K-Mart "blue-light special" long after she could have securely shopped at Macy's. In my family, you never asked what something cost. I knew my mother handled the family finances, but I had no clue what that involved.

My first memory of church and money (not counting the nickel I dropped in the weekly collection plate) is from when I was about six. It was probably in Sunday school at the Baptist Church I went to with a friend—my parents never went to church, so I just tagged along with whoever was my best friend at the time. I was invited to come up on the stage with two other children. One of us was given a nickel and the other a copy of the New Testament. I was asked if I would rather have the nickel to buy a doll or have "The Word of God." Even in my state of arrested financial development I knew dolls cost more than a nickel! Besides, Mamma didn't raise no fool! I dutifully chose the book, though I would have preferred the nickel. Then the adult told me to open the back cover, and taped to its inside was a shiny new dime! Hallelujah, I was saved!

My next memorable experience had to do with pledging just after I had joined the Congregational Church with my ninth grade confirmation class. (We had moved and now my new best friend was Congregational.) They handed out cards asking how much we would give with not much explanation of the meaning of the word *pledge.* I knew that if I filled out the card I would get one of those nifty boxes with little envelopes inside. So I pledged $52, figuring that I'd drop a buck in the plate each Sunday. Well, the end of the year rolled around. I had not been to the church service every Sunday (I taught Sunday school instead), and sometimes I forgot my cute little envelopes and just dropped the dollar in the plate. In the mail came a notice that I owed the church a huge sum of money. I was stunned! Even cute envelopes couldn't entice me after that. And I'm not sure I ever officially paid off that pledge.

When I joined the Unitarian Universalist Church in New Orleans nearly thirty years later, nothing much had changed. Money wasn't mentioned much there either. We weren't given pledge cards until the canvass occurred, nearly six months after we had signed the book. Some discussion of the budget took place at the annual congregational meeting, but we received no guidelines for giving. The implication was that nothing much was expected. I don't think our congregation was very different from most Unitarian Universalist churches. And the poor results at the end of the canvass highlighted a serious flaw in the system.

As I think about the fourteen years I've been a Unitarian Universalist, my personal increase in comfort with financial issues mirrors a cultural change in our church. I first became aware of the intricacies of church finances as a board member, particularly when we had to deal with the annual problem of summer's low cash flow. We realized the problem was never going away if we did not seriously educate the congregation about the realities of running this business we called "First Church." It was then that we instituted an important cultural change and vowed that finances and money would be talked about openly all year long, not just at canvass time or when there was a money crisis and we needed to beg.

Other changes occurred slowly: official quarterly financial reports to the congregation, reminders *before* the summer slump to keep pledges up-to-date (or ahead for those people going on extended vacations), discussions from the pulpit about money as it relates to spirituality (not just on canvass Sunday), and major changes in the annual canvass drive. This included a commitment to face-to-face canvassing (by the book), publishing charts and expected giving tables in the canvass brochure, and short testimonials from members on Sundays about the importance of this church community and why they give generously. We even had people at canvass time sharing their actual pledge amounts with each other—a giant step!

There is one theory that canvass time should just be about money, and canvassers should be straightforward and direct. Ask for the money and don't dilute the process with other things. There may be some validity to this theory, but I think it is too narrow a view of money and the canvass. For people to see the relationship between money and other aspects of church life, they need to be discussed together: money and programming, money and building community, money and maintaining the church facilities, money and a highly qualified professional staff and, not least, money and our personal spiritual life.

Our yearly campaign broadened the meaning of *canvass* from a mere pledge drive to include canvassing for ideas, interests, and constructive criticism. We made a commitment that the information we collected would be passed on to the appropriate person/committee and not languish somewhere in a forgotten file drawer! Not only did we obtain some very useful information, but the canvassers were much more comfortable with the process. Because having a questionnaire to help break the ice made canvassing less threatening, finding volunteers was much easier.

As we changed the way we dealt with church finances and our canvass drives, we started seeing higher pledges. People were being listened to and felt that their money was being handled responsibly. I was growing along with my church. As a board member I reluctantly had agreed to canvass. It was expected! I was as uncomfortable as everyone else. But with the new process, I discovered that canvassing was even fun! I got to meet new people and make contact with long-term members I didn't know so well. Some of those connections still remain strong.

My presidency of the congregation marked a milestone in my growth as a lay leader and in the growth of the church. We were deciding what to do about our shabby, nonaccessible, too-crowded facility. This certainly challenged all my leadership skills. While we had come a long way toward fiscal responsibility, we still struggled yearly to meet our budget, and the thought of raising lots of money in a capital campaign was very scary. An architect offered suggestions for how we could maximize our use of space and upgrade the building on our tiny lot. Even the best scenario left us little room for growth. Then a church eight blocks up the street sprouted a For Sale sign.

We visited and immediately knew it was meant to be ours. We recognized that this move wouldn't cost much more than renovating. It was a long, complicated, sometimes painful process that took us two and one-half years. Yet some magical things happened along the way.

The day we finally decided to sell our church, make the purchase, and begin the capital campaign, the vote was almost unanimous—only one "no" vote and one abstention. The long-term member who abstained came up to me afterward to explain. She said that as sad as it made her to think of leaving our old building, she really understood that for the future of our church it was a necessary move and she supported the decision. But she knew that this vote meant the congregation was taking on a large financial burden. She wasn't in a position to give much money to this project, so she didn't feel she had the right to vote for it. This woman, who had raised her children in this church, who had taught Sunday school, who arranged flowers, who had pledged as generously as her circumstances permitted, who spent untold hours doing the little things no one ever notices (washing tablecloths, cleaning out kitchen cupboards)—this woman felt she didn't have the right to vote! How sad that we give this much power to money. I told her that I understood her feelings and appreciated her concerns, but that if anyone in this group had earned a right to vote on this issue certainly she had. This was probably the beginning of my "money ministry."

In the struggle toward the move, I longed to be part of a church with a nice fat endowment fund. Since then I have moderated my feelings about this. In my travels and conversations with Unitarian Universalists across the country, I've discovered that some of our most stagnant congregations have large endowments. Of course many churches with large endowments are vital, growing congregations and do wonderful, generous things.

Some wealthy churches do not even conduct an annual canvass, instead relying on their past to support their church and its programs. This is a great disservice to the present generation. Generous giving is an experience people need to cultivate and our churches can provide. It is also an experience we need to pass on to our children by including them in appropriate ways. The very process a group goes through in raising money, if done well, can provide healthy and revitalizing challenges for both the church community and individuals within it. And the lack of those challenges can prove deadly. I once belonged to a nonprofit educational organization that put on conferences and workshops for educators and school administrators. Although the activities were educationally successful, we were in debt most of the time. As long as we were in debt, our activities continued and were otherwise successful. But one day we found ourselves running in the black and were delighted. The pressure was off, and a short time later the organization died. Looking back, I think the need to raise money was part of the glue that held us together.

Raising money, particularly in a large capital campaign, can unite a congregation in a way not many other activities can. The planning process itself can be a wondrously revitalizing time. It involves revisiting (or sometimes creating) the church mission statement to ensure that the congregation has a sense of common direction and purpose. The process of planning a building or remodeling project refines church goals. If a congregation is truly program driven, it will need to work through its priorities before deciding how to proceed with the physical space. When a church carefully looks at who it is and what it wants to be, health comes. And by the time you get to the money part, you are likely to have an excited, enthusiastically committed group of people ready to turn their dreams into realities.

Even the process of asking the congregation to dig deep into their pockets to fund their dreams can have spiritual dimensions. Remember the woman in my congregation who abstained? Her story didn't end there. She had been retired for many years but a one-year job in her specialty came up to fill in for someone on sabbatical. She took the job with the thought that now she would be able to make a generous contribution to our capital campaign! She is my hero. Her ministry, though she never would think of it this way, inspired me and many others in the church. I am reminded of the biblical story of "The Widow's Mite" in which Jesus is entering the temple with his disciples. He points out the rich man tossing a couple of gold coins in the plate and then the impoverished crone dropping in a few pennies, and he asks which has given more. Some people in our congregation gave larger sums to the campaign, but none gave more of themselves than she. How often do we get such chances to be heroes, to be ministers? And how often do we rise to the occasion?

I went on to cochair the capital campaign. Working with a fundraising consultant, I realized that what we were learning for this particular campaign was going to carry on into the future of this congregation, and, I would discover later, into my own future. This campaign was not just about raising money. It was about dreaming and making those dreams come true. We discovered that if we worked together as a congregation, we could reach further and do more than any one of us ever thought possible. We also learned that everyone's contribution was important. The large gifts were glitzy and exciting, but the bulk of the money came from the average person, and even the most modest gifts were necessary to reach our goal.

After so much hard work and community effort, we celebrated our move in traditional New Orleans style, with a brass band and a parade from the old church to the new.

I realized that I actually enjoyed working with church finances and fundraising campaigns, and I had some leadership skills in this area. So when I was offered a job by the UUA to work with churches around the country I was delighted. I was going to become a minister—someone the dictionary defines as one who "gives care or aid" and "contributes, as to comfort or happiness." I like that a lot!

My work helps this liberal religion that I love grow on a congregational level. Congregations can better reach out to new members and to the needs of their communities if they have new or bigger or updated buildings, new Sunday school space, better accessibility for the differently abled, and a sense of being able to do BIG things (which can be one of the side benefits of successfully completing a capital campaign).

On an individual level, I hope that my work enables people to confront some of their issues with the dreaded $^\$M^\$$ word, become more comfortable talking about money, and develop a true spirit of stewardship for their churches, communities, and the world.

~

Jeri Moulder is a member of the Unitarian Society of Santa Barbara. Currently she is a Fundraising Consultant for the UUA, does leadership consulting for churches, and serves on the Board of Trustees for The Mountain.

Ten Myths of Leadership

Helen Bishop

A healthy concept of shared ministry contradicts ten myths we commonly hold about leadership:

Leaders are born, not made.
This is the "Great Man/Great Woman" school of leadership studies. Adherents develop lists of traits shared by leaders and put together ways of identifying people who have those traits. They come up with checklists, inventories for self-knowledge, and materials designed to help people find out what they were born with. This approach lends itself to finding out whether someone is charismatic and has high energy levels, but it's not so good at developing leadership skills—for example, being able to analyze a situation, defining and communicating a sense of vision, persistence, rising above the fray for a long-range perspective, and the willingness to take risks.

Leaders are people who persuade followers to do what the leader wants.
An iron fist in a velvet glove is still hard underneath. I prefer to think that leaders and followers *do* leadership together. They spend quite a bit of time talking things over to determine their mutual purposes, so that the changes they undertake reflect the insights of both leaders and followers.

Leadership and management are the same thing.
The rule here is, "Managers do things right. Leaders do the right thing." Both statements are simplistic. The key to leadership is *change*. If nothing needs to be changed, management processes are more appropriate. In case you think leadership is more important than management, imagine trying to keep your life in order when you never know when your paycheck will arrive!

Situational leadership is possible.
Some leadership practitioners spend time with charts and graphs, trying to determine the maturity of the group and its members, the need in the group for close supervision versus autonomy, and the group's norms for managing conflict and decision making. Then they use their findings to tailor their oversight of individuals and the group as a whole. It is important for leaders to acquire a considerable amount of expertise in assessing and managing group processes, but I haven't found a simple chart or graph that serves me well in matching my leadership style to group tasks and processes.

Leadership can be done in one-minute bursts.
This school of thought describes short, intense bursts of interaction which will modify behaviors and keep things on an even keel. In my own experience, leadership requires time, care, and attention—and one minute is grossly insufficient to affect leadership processes.

The leader is the person at the top.
Leadership can be thought of as a dance, with no set rules for who leads when. Leadership can be found anywhere— in the mail room, at the secretary's desk, in the supply room, in the person of the custodian as well as the chief executive officer. Many things are easier if you have resources such as time, money, the ability to set and evaluate an agenda, and personnel. But leaders and followers can work together to mobilize these kinds of resources. In fact, leaders and followers frequently change places as the leadership progresses.

A leader works alone.
Real leaders work in networks of people who share common values, agree on the mission and vision of the project, and are willing to devote resources of time, energy, money, attention, and skill to creating and implementing changes that align with the common vision. These networks can be geographically limited, but as the complexity of the change process increases, so does the size of the network. Someone working alone is a person working alone. Leaders and followers do leadership together.

Discussing "values" in connection with "leadership" is a contradiction.
Shared values are one of the hallmarks of a group doing leadership. Sometimes leaders and followers disagree on instrumental values, such as how to get there, but they agree on terminal values—where they are trying to go. A key leadership role is the articulation of common, shared values.

A good leader works hard, takes responsibility for the outcome, and has no personal life.
True, a leader works hard and devotes many resources, including time, to the project or change at hand. But most change processes are lengthy, and the implementation phase can be the trickiest and most complex part of the entire project. Leaders and followers need persistence, they need to be committed to the long haul. Leaders spend a good deal of time cheerleading, keeping people's spirits up in the face of opposition or derailment. This long perspective requires that a leader practice good self-care. Leaders must take breathers, time away, and must build in time to pay attention to their personal lives, including family and friends. The goal is to work toward changes that reflect mutual purposes, not to burn people up like toast.

The "vision thing" is a side issue.
It is the vision of mutual purposes that keeps leaders and followers doing leadership, not a flash-in-the-pan desire to be a big shot. Change processes are lengthy, messy, some-

times tedious and perplexing, sometimes scary, always risky. Everyone sharing the common vision, leaders and followers both, has something to contribute, which in this context we call *shared ministry*. Ministry lies in the heart of the congregation, not just in the heart of an individual.

Here's a story of leadership: Once upon a time, as all stories should begin, a Unitarian Universalist layperson took it into her head to become more active in her church. "Where can I get some training in how to be a church leader?" she asked a member of the board. "Well," said the board member, "a good place to start would be to take a look at your gifts and talents, so we can see how best to strengthen your sense of ministry within our congregation."

The board member found a copy of the self-assessment instrument distributed every spring as part of the canvass process and gave it to the layperson, who filled it out and put in the mailbox of the board member, who called her back the following week. "Seems to me," said the board member, "that your ministry lies in the area of religious education. Let me connect you up with the director of our religious education program; he'll be *delighted* to hear of your interest."

Sure enough, the director called the layperson a few days later. He described the RE program's vision of helping children and youth develop a sense of Unitarian Universalist identity through carefully structured curricula and projects, both within the church and in the larger community. "We offer training every spring for people who would like to share in this ministry to children and youth," the director said. "We'll cover the parameters of the program, and would like to invite you to join the religious education committee starting in June with the committee retreat."

"How would committee work help me with leadership?" the layperson asked. "Good question," said the director. "Come with me to the next RE committee meeting, and you can get a feel for this ministry."

So the following Wednesday, the layperson arranged child care for her own children, and showed up at the church at 7:00 pm. The director met her at the door, introduced her to the chair and other members of the committee, handed her a name tag with letters big enough to read across the room, gave her a folder containing the minutes of the last three meetings and the agenda for this meeting, and invited her to grab something to drink before the meeting started.

The chairperson asked everyone to find a seat and began the meeting by reading an inspiring passage from a meditation manual. He invited people to check in, and committee members took a few minutes to talk about their lives outside the church—their partners and spouses, children and grandchildren and pets, job stresses, plumbing disasters, and upcoming minor surgeries.

The chair asked for an approval of the agenda, went over the ground rules for meetings which the committee had approved at its last retreat (speaking for oneself, allowing quiet people time to speak if they wanted to, no interruptions or put-downs, speaking directly to the person involved if you're in conflict with someone), added two items of new business, and requested approval of the times allotted for each item. The layperson left the meeting at 9:00 p.m. in plenty of time to take the baby sitter home, feeling connected with the committee and with the RE program.

The layperson served on the RE committee for three years, and during that time, the director made sure she knew of workshops, seminars, and training opportunities in the church and in the district. The layperson got over her butterflies at making public presentations and facilitated a workshop for youth advisors in her first year on the committee. She distributed the evaluation forms that the director had given her, and participants rated her workshop "good" and "excellent" except for pacing, which was a little slow. She revised her timings a little and presented the workshop again at the district annual meeting. This time, participants rated everything "good" or "excellent."

"Well done!" said the director when he saw the evaluations. "Can you chair the task force evaluating the youth program this year? We'll use the same forms we used last year, and you'll need to set up a meeting for parents and caregivers, to be sure people have the opportunity to let us know how things are going. The committee chair will work on it with you, and one other person in the congregation indicated an interest in evaluating religious education programs. You'd need to prepare a report for the committee when you've completed the evaluation process;

that gives you two months before the committee meeting where we reflect on how the program has gone this year. I'll be happy to serve as a resource—can you take this on?"

"I'm—I'm surprised that you trust me with such an important process," said the layperson, "but yes, I think I can do it. Can I call you if I get stuck?" "Sure," said the director, "and I'll check in with you a couple of times in the first two weeks or so, just to see how things are going. Thanks for saying yes. You're making quite a valuable contribution to the program here."

The layperson found it interesting to look at the goals for the youth program and compare them with reports from youth, parents, and advisors. She announced two meetings for parents, one after church and the other on a weeknight, and met with youth during their regularly scheduled program. She distributed a form to the advisors, and she met with them over pizza and soda once she'd heard from youth, parents, and caregivers. There she listened to the advisors, and she was able to give them some feedback about the program before she completed the final report. The committee chair facilitated one of the parent meetings, and she and the congregation member worked together on the final report.

The committee expressed great appreciation to the task force when the final report was submitted, and used it as the basis for setting goals for the following year. "Well," said the director, "how would you like your contribution to be recognized by the church?" "What do you mean?" asked the layperson. "Well, every year we have a Volunteer

Recognition Sunday, where everyone involved in the shared ministry of the congregation gets a flower and an invitation to brunch prepared and served by members of the board. Some people don't like that kind of public recognition, though. One person on the religious education committee likes being invited to a brown-bag lunch with the minister; someone else wants a note from me, but doesn't want her name included in the order of service on Volunteer Sunday. What's your pleasure?"

"Thanks for asking," said the layperson. "I travel a lot for work, and what I'd really like is a $5 gift certificate I can use at the book stall, since I'm always going through my meager supply of paperbacks to read on planes. Is that the sort of thing you mean?" "Sure," said the director, and he noted her request on the little notepad he carried in his pocket. He also told the layperson about an upcoming weekend training session on the philosophy of religious education, and informed her that scholarships were available through the church and the district RE committee.

The layperson received her gift certificate, went to the philosophy training module, and went on to chair the religious education committee at the church. She also joined the district RE committee, which she chaired in due course. She ended up attending all seven of the religious education training modules and received a lapel pin in recognition of her accomplishment.

The layperson came to enjoy planning and giving workshops, and she became a regular presenter at the district annual meeting. That's how she came to the attention of a staff person from the Unitarian Universalist Association, who attended a workshop and was impressed. When she returned to headquarters in Boston, the staff member contacted the layperson and asked her if she'd be willing to co-lead one of the religious education modules, with the idea of becoming a full-fledged leader the next time around. By this time, the layperson had become quite comfortable leading workshops, so she said "Yes" and became a leader for three of the modules.

In addition, her reputation as a presenter got her an invitation to lead a workshop at the UUA General Assembly, so she attended as a delegate from her church. She agreed to serve on the board of her congregation, thereby getting to know the coministers of this large church on a different level than she had when she was one of hundreds of people sitting in the pews.

In her spare time, she completed an advanced degree in curriculum design and educational technology, and another in organizational development. When the district board chair asked her to consider running for the board, she said, "Yes." That's where she saw a flier for a position as a district executive.

The district wanted someone with considerable background and experience in religious education, as well as in organizational development and other aspects of congregational life. When she applied for the position, both the Association and the district were impressed with her credentials, and she became the district executive for a Midwestern district, where she's living happily ever after.

Can this story be true? The answer of course is yes. Some of the details have been altered a bit for continuity, but the heart of the story is true, and the layperson is me. I hope you enjoy the practice of leadership in shared ministry as much as I have!

~

Helen Bishop, who earned her master's degree in educational technology and a doctorate in organizational leadership, became the Central Midwest District Administrator in July 1992. She is currently part of a team developing new training resources to strengthen and revitalize healthy congregations.

Multiplying Ministry

Ardath Schaibly

I was a reluctant newcomer to First Unitarian Universalist Church of San Diego years ago. The sumptuous programs there attracted me, but I was reluctant to become involved. Truthfully, I was tired from my leadership load at the small fellowship we'd come from, and I wanted a rest. Besides, I was anxious about meeting what I imagined as higher expectations in this more sophisticated sphere. I missed the cozy intimacy of the fellowship, the comfort of knowing everybody at the social hour.

I may have been reluctant, but I kept coming. Some of the ways I had contributed at my old fellowship were covered here by first-rate paid staff. I wasn't sure I could make a contribution, but I stayed around because I needed the church. As a parent drawn by the religious education program, I started to help in small ways and to make friends there.

Eventually I plunged into the inner workings of the church, which opened up a new world to me. It's one thing to sit in the audience and enjoy a performance, and quite another to go backstage and help put it on. I discovered the engines powering the programs, maintaining the infrastructure, serving the members in this large church. Here I contributed my amateur energy in new spheres of business, finance, education, social action, and more, realms beyond my reach in the outside world. I learned new concepts and skills working alongside professionals, and I carried these skills outside the church into my world. Undergirding the risk of experimentation was the personal and spiritual support of my church community. It has all been a religious experience. And it continues today.

First Unitarian Universalist Church's modeling of shared leadership begins with our coministers, the Reverends Tom and Carolyn Owen-Towle, and spreads throughout the church community. Opportunities for lay involvement and leadership extend through many spheres of our church's life, particularly religious education, administration, community building, worship support, and social action. The committee is the key vehicle for performing the work of the church, and at last count, we had over eighty of them. Over the past fifteen years, I've served on at least twenty-five.

While we have excellent staff, volunteer support keeps the church going. Widespread sharing of responsibility for church activities is characteristic of our philosophy of congregational well-being. New members are urged to get involved right away, so as to meet more people and invest themselves for a higher return. For members to connect, make friends, and find a place, the large church must promote interaction in small groups.

How do we share leadership? We pass power around. Though many busy workers pursue and coordinate specialized activities, our volunteers do not follow precise roles, nor are they expected to retain the same responsibilities or serve on the same committees forever. We encourage teamwork and flexibility. We teach and help each other, and we value everyone's contribution.

To assist in training and continuity, large committees tend to be cochaired and to have staggered terms. Elected officers and board trustees have term limits with the church president automatically moving through vice president, president, and past president positions. The board and other large committees schedule annual retreats to build teamwork. Our budget subsidizes attendance at our district leadership training school for trustees and other leaders. Workshops, handbooks, and curriculum guides help to plug in people as they learn by doing.

Everybody is recruited for something, and the recruitment takes many forms. A personal invitation to join a specific committee honors the individual, and it may be an offer one cannot refuse. Sermons spur on new commitment and remind us that as we give, we receive. A yearly volunteer fair advertises slots that need filling. Short-term tasks may hook in someone from the periphery and connect people with similar interests. Nominating committees search for proven talent to fill the really big jobs. Most church officials start small and grow through the ranks, flourishing in several fields and proving their worthiness as faithful servants before they are elected.

In our church, shared leadership is growing into the concept of shared ministry. Tom and Carolyn themselves exemplify shared ministry, and now we are extending the concept beyond position to function—first by recognizing the role of the director of religious education as a ministry. Beyond that grows a vision of expanding ministry from pulpit through pews, empowering the laity to minister to each other.

How does the laity minister? Consider the minister. Through example and message, ministers inspire, strengthen, comfort, and celebrate to help us to grow deeper spiritually, taller personally, and wider communally. Tom and Carolyn lavishly minister to us in the way they model coministry, commitment to action, and dedicated service. As personal coaches, they raise the hurdles and cheer, and as spiritual teachers they open windows of the heart to the universe. Tom and Carolyn are catalysts for ministry within the congregation. Involvement in our web of community carries the expectation that members will pitch in to work together. Tom and Carolyn ask us to minister to them as well, to care for them as people.

Our lay ministry means we care for and celebrate one another, we teach and encourage each other, we inspire and motivate. When we share what we have with others, ministry is multiplied. When we represent Unitarian Universalism to the world, we are ministering. When we march for minority rights, we are ministering. When we demonstrate our values, we minister. When religion is your life, you are a minister. We are a welcoming church, developing an intentionally diverse religious community. We are a loving church, embracing our family and encouraging them to grow. We are a teaching church, helping to grow ministers, including those in the intern minister program. Ministry is shared in all the church's programs.

Like me, many volunteers get their feet wet in religious education programs. When our son was small, I helped out in his classrooms, providing snacks, stories, and crafts. As he grew, I did, too, planning curricula and learning new games. Both of us made friends. When our son reached his teens, his father and I befriended his peer group and joined in their guidance. Religious education is a family matter, a church family matter, not to be left in the hands of a few. With able direction by a professional staff person, teams of leaders are recruited, trained, and coordinated to teach Sunday classes for all children and youth. Rotating teams spread the responsibility and multiply the experience gained. We look to more than just parents to fill leader teams. Many adults are rewarded by the company of children and vice versa.

Teams of capable, indefatigable adults can help facilitate programs that empower youth to develop self-esteem and healthy peer groups. These are challenging years for teens and their parents, as teens wrestle with ideas, identity, and values. Our high school group gives life-changing support to youth. The years I taught and coordinated "About Your Sexuality" classes may have been my most valuable contribution as a volunteer.

Religious education never stops. Many opportunities for adults to learn and share what they know are offered through our extensive adult education program. Members with special expertise or creative ideas lead workshops in a wide variety of subjects. Church orientation classes usually led by ministers may be given by seasoned members.

As a large church, we hire a lot of help, but it takes volunteers to run the business. Most of our superb employees are church members who started out as volunteers. Along with the ordained ministers, our church administrator is a key operator of the organization. With wide responsibilities in church business and an experienced, comprehensive view, the administrator is a major source of information and advice for church leaders and a powerful model of professional, practical, and personal skills. The church as a business serves its investors, and it provides people, space, and materials for getting things done. Effective communicating, information processing, recordkeeping, and scheduling are required for the smooth and efficient operation of the church.

As I served on various church committees, I learned about personnel relations, evaluations and compensations, regulations and negotiations. I became involved in hiring and management. I learned how to read financial reports and to solicit contributions. By collaborating with volunteers of different backgrounds, I learned from them and applied my experience to a new setting. It is rewarding to work in a religious climate of respect and affirmation, for that is the business of the church.

Volunteers decide how our church business will operate, how to better utilize and preserve our resources of people. We survey the congregation, hold forums and focus groups to involve laity in long-range planning and developing a vision for the church. Volunteers decide where the church is going.

The board of trustees represents the laity as elected decision makers. Trustees are selected to serve as pillars in the church structure. The board exercises corporate power to provide facilities, funds, and staff, make policy, appoint committees, and recommend action. Few of us wield such authority in the commercial world. It is a heavy responsibility. As stewards of a large not-for-profit organization, church officers hold positions comparable to business executives or government officials, and they do it without compensation, but not without reward. For me, serving as church president was a supreme honor and a tremendous challenge, a completely unexpected chance to grow.

How does a large church create an intimate family feeling? A lot of what happens in our church stretches beyond Sunday and past the property line. My husband and I belong to a church neighborhood group, whose primary purpose is to give each other emotional support. We meet monthly for potlucks in members' homes.

In bereavement and other hard times we have been comforted most by caring friends in church circles. Counselors lead services of healing which Carolyn designed so that troubled persons could unburden themselves in a safe, small group setting. A caregivers network was organized to provide temporary assistance to members in emergencies. Being able to help someone who really appreciates it boosts the caregiver, too.

Activities designed for fun also light up our church community. Holiday parties that involve wearing Halloween costumes, trimming a Christmas tree, and decorating Easter eggs have brought out the child in me. Annual retreats invigorate participants and develop leadership skills. Lay leaders carry the primary responsibility for these programs which result in so many affirming, enriching experiences.

When the laity comes out of the pews and up to the podium, we witness a powerful aspect of shared ministry. Lay leaders routinely assist in conducting worship services. Special theme services involve multiple lay speakers, co-ordinated by a minister. Both the Men's Fellowship and the Women's Federation conduct annual Sunday services. Lay-led summer services are typically presented by church groups, such as the gay-lesbian outreach. These services are well-prepared and well-attended.

A giant step toward empowerment of laity was the addition of personal credos to worship services. In these, members tell about their own lives, revealing significant events and influences, expressing their current guiding religious values. These credos make impressive, influential statements in conjunction with a minister's sermon. For the speaker, the experience of reflecting on one's beliefs is valuable and challenging. The credos also provide a meaningful way of introducing more people to the large church community.

We are an intergenerational community. Children regularly attend worship services, and they lead rituals, light candles, perform music, and otherwise share in conducting worship. Children and youth present special programs. A moving worship service culminates our All Church Camp after a weekend on the mountain at deBenneville Pines. In the worship, people offer their appreciation of the setting and of experiences that have bonded the campers. We recall the contributions, the creations and conversations, the rituals and reminiscences that lift our souls. Nature and music and the beautiful people bring poetry to my heart and inspire me to speak.

Music is a vital part of worship, extending the spiritual and aesthetic dimensions. Our church has an outstanding, diverse music program expertly directed by the professional staff. Services feature special music by professional or lay soloists, our strong church choir, and folk guitar ensemble. Whether we lift our voices together in hymns or hootenannies, music joins our spirits. An exceptional volunteer coordinates a long-standing concert series which draws the public. Volunteers developed our children's choir. In promoting the goal of cultural diversity, some members sing with an interfaith gospel choir. Immense volunteer efforts even sent our choir on tour in Transylvania.

The Sunday service is the most visible focus of church activity and there are so many ways that volunteers contribute—organizing ushers, creating floral displays, managing the sound system, serving at coffee hour, and more.

We are grateful for our artists, interior designers, and others who provide the thousand details that grace the whole experience.

Social action committees attract volunteers who want to take a stand for their values and make a difference in the world beyond their church. Volunteers may initiate projects, or a minister may jump-start a project, then let it roll by momentum as volunteers guide it down the road. Our social action committee energized participation by restructuring into separate task forces, a divide-and-multiply maneuver that increased effectiveness in eight areas and expanded opportunities for leadership. While some volunteers engage in compassionate charitable activities such as helping people with AIDS and collecting for food drives, others advocate reforms and tackle issues such as preserving the environment and protecting reproductive rights. Volunteers are busy doing everything from arranging public forums to raising organic gardens. The church annually hosts a homeless shelter program which needs overnight chaperones, cooks, transportation crews, and so on. Our high school group undertakes ambitious projects such as crossing the border to lay tile in a school being built in a poor Mexican neighborhood.

Social activist leaders draw attention to causes needing protest and reform. Though churches may not engage in political activity, individuals may motivate members to act. Tom inspired me to join a task force that works to preserve First Amendment religious freedom and civil liberties in our pluralistic society. I publish a news bulletin to help inform the community on the issue and build a network of volunteers. This task requires me to leap into new worlds of information and technical skills. My church community empowered me to express my religious principles, to take a stand and make a difference, and I am sustained by loyal supporters who assist me on the team.

In all these activities of the church, volunteers learn by doing. We pick up all sorts of practical skills and professional tips from working with others who have more experience. I learned computer word processing because I needed it for church. My husband learned budgeting and construction skills as a church volunteer. As a private person, I gained more confidence by going public. Involvement is empowering. In my church I feel power in the presence of a common identity unifying our diversity. As a minority of religious liberals, Unitarian Universalists thrive by banding together. We keep good company. We walk on the spiritual path with ministers, mentors, and models who inspire us.

We show up at church with our simple desire to be useful and to please others, to fulfill our duty and to express love. We may want to belong, to receive recognition, or to feel challenged. We respond to invitation and friendly persuasion or to general expectations. We are rewarded by recognition and a sense of accomplishment. The motivations and rewards of volunteer involvement reinforce the individual and the church.

As volunteers grow, the church grows too, inside and out. Just recently several church members rose to ordained ministry. Others started up new congregations. More volunteers took roles in district and national leadership. In our church many lead and even more come to help. We learn as we share our ministry, guided by our church affirmation, "May love be the spirit of this church, . . . and service be its prayer."

~

Ardath Schaibly embraced Unitarian Universalism in Michigan over thirty years ago. Along with teaching and family counseling, she has made a career of volunteering with her church family in San Diego.

~ Serving Many Well

Ministry to Each Other Comes First

Roger W. Comstock

People don't join a church to do the work or pay the bills; they join to get something of value for themselves and their families. But the most important resource any church has is its volunteers, and when you see a church in which the members have begun to lose interest in doing the work, you are looking at a church that is in decline and will close sooner or later.

This creates a dilemma. The volunteers are the members, too, and for the most part, they are members before they become volunteers. Only after they have joined and begun to benefit from the services that a church offers will members want to support that community with their effort and their money.

The act of joining a church is an act of covenanting, or it should be. We Unitarian Universalists don't require adherence to any specific doctrine or faith, but we do require adherence to the principle that each of us is free to seek truth for him- or herself in the context of religious community. That, combined with our adherence to the democratic process and to congregational polity, constitutes our covenant with each other.

When a new member joins, she or he agrees to honor that covenant. The new member is really making a number of promises—to participate in the life of the church, attend services, be present when the community makes decisions, help each other, and help with the work and the financial responsibility. I think it leads to a stronger membership bond if this covenant is articulated explicitly.

In recent years, we have not been good about articulating our expectations of members, new and old. "Just sign a card and toss it on the secretary's desk," my wife and I were once told when we inquired about membership. This is not the way to signify membership. We need to make the act of joining mean something, and this act ought to be attended to at the time it happens and later, in a liturgical way, shared with the whole congregation at a Sunday service. If the act of joining is viewed as a commitment on the part of one member to all the others, then the idea of legislating membership or financial requirements in the bylaws becomes uncomfortable.

Good recruiting starts with intentionality. Figure out what the job is. What are its tasks and limits? Is it a one-time task, or one that will continue over a period of time? If it is the latter, such as being the chair of a committee, how long will the job last? How many meetings are involved and how often? How will the volunteer find the necessary resources—money, people, and space—to do the job? Why is this job important in the life of the church?

Then figure out who would be the best person for the job. Do you need an organizer or a facilitator, a caretaker or a teacher, a technician or a worker? What skill sets are needed? Can it be done alone, or will it involve working with others? Does it entail a knowledge of the church and its organizational politics? Does it involve motivating others or recruiting? Is there someone new who would contribute if asked?

When I look for key people—potential district officers and board members—the two qualities I seek are a positive attitude (a willingness to try new things, to be creative) and the ability to work cooperatively with others.

Successful recruiting takes preparation. It is better to phone someone than to approach them in church. It is better to meet face-to-face than to talk on the phone. It is better to take the time and effort to meet privately than to make the approach casually. Be prepared. Figure out how you might help this person take the job; for example, know people who might help, assist in recruiting, provide training, and so on. Know why you have chosen this particular person for the job and be ready to tell her or him. Think through what this person's concerns may be and have answers ready. Highlight the strong points he or she will bring. Invite questions. Don't insist on an answer right away.

Remember that the act of recruiting implies a compliment. Don't apologize or act embarrassed. "I think you are the right person for this job" is more effective than "Is there anyone out there who. . . ?" In my opinion, broadcast advertising for key jobs is counterproductive. The church that puts a notice in the newsletter asking if there is anyone willing to take on the denominational affairs chairpersonship is asking for trouble. This is admitting that it hasn't been easy to find someone, and is saying, in effect, this job isn't important enough to seek out the very best.

Successful recruiting requires that you recognize and acknowledge why people want to work for the church—to grow and learn, to provide a needed service, to satisfy the need to serve, to work and interact with others in the faith community. Know and be able to name these motivations. The church offers many unique opportunities to grow and develop, opportunities often not available to us at work or at home. Public speaking, fundraising, long-range planning, service—these all are tasks that church offers us.

If you've chosen your recruit carefully, then you've approached someone for whom this assignment is a challenge and an opportunity. If family considerations, work, or other factors dictate that the person can't take it on right now, be gracious and leave the door open: "I understand why you can't do it right now, but I'd like to be able to ask you again in the future when things change."

Once a person is recruited, what then? It is common in our churches to just let them go and expect them to do a good job. When I recruit someone to do a key job, I regard that agreement as a two-way contract. The volunteer's part of the contract is clear; my part of the contract is less clear but just as important. When I ask someone to do a job, I take on the responsibility to help the recruit succeed at the task, that is, to observe what is happening, to answer questions, to offer suggestions, to help in finding resources, to give encouragement, appreciation, and feedback. It is my job to empower those who have agreed to work for me.

In the church, we have many chances to think about the welfare of the individual versus the accomplishment of the task. In my view, the relationship must always come first, followed by getting the job done. If the leadership handles it well, doing the job is a part of making the relationship right. The essential ingredient in leadership is trust. Trust happens when relationships are real and mutually respectful, if not satisfying. Trust happens when we tell the truth, even if it hurts. Trust happens when we honor our commitments.

When thinking about a job to do, our church leaders often think in terms of the work, not the people. "Where can we find someone to do this job?" If we remember that we are about doing ministry among each other first and foremost, if we focus on the people and not on the work, we can go a long way toward having an effective church organization.

We can drift into thinking there's not enough to go around, enough help, enough money, enough anything. This attitude of scarcity limits our vision. But when the leadership creates the vision and empowers the members, the resources appear. Let me illustrate with a story.

In the late 1980s, a lay-led fellowship in Macon, Georgia, had about fifty members who met each Sunday in the basement of a bank. The children held their religious education program in the furnace room. For years the fellowship had struggled with the question, "Should we buy a building, or should we get a minister?" They couldn't get off the fence. Some wanted a building, others thought the minister was more important. Many feared there wasn't enough money for either. Finally one strong leader said, "Why don't we get a building and a minister?" He convinced them to try. That was in the winter of 1987. By the following fall, they had located a building for sale for $100,000 and moved in to share it with the previous owners while that group finished their new space. At the same time, the fellowship applied for Extension Ministry. It was approved, and they had a half-time minister by January 1988. By that summer, they had purchased the building and paid off three-quarters of its cost and had been able to move the minister to full-time. Today the membership is three times what it was in early 1987, and the group is thriving and growing. Someone put forth a vision the members could buy, they got excited and supportive, the church grew, and the resources were found.

When a church board says to me, "We'll do it if we can find the money," my response is: "If you first have to have the money before you can articulate the vision, you will decide not to do it." People respond to a vision. People respond when their needs for growth and service and community are met in the church. It is leadership's job to find ways of accomplishing that empowerment.

When I was thinking about applying to be a district

executive with the Unitarian Universalist Association, one of the people I talked with was Gene Pickett. He was the UUA president at the time, but I consulted him because he had been my minister in Atlanta and I trusted his advice. "You seem to have all the right qualifications," he said. "What worries you?" "Doing sermons," I said. "As a layman, I don't have any experience with Sunday services. I'm not sure I have anything to say anyone else would want to hear."

"Good!" That's all he said.

That one word said many things to me. It said, "Good. If you're unsure, you will take it seriously and probably do a better job." It said, "Good. I know you can do it." It said, "Try it, you'll like it." It said, "Good. I think you have something to say." It gave me the courage to try writing and delivering a sermon, even though the first one was a disaster. Probably, I would have learned to do sermons anyway, but Gene's clear confidence in me helped at a time when I was taking on a significant new challenge. That was some of the most empowering advice I ever received.

Here's a third story of empowerment. A 100-member congregation had been meeting in rented space and wanted to find their own quarters, but they could not find a suitable building. Just as they were about to give up, an existing church decided to move and put their building on the market for $250,000. The congregation's leaders visited the property. Though it was bigger than they needed, they liked it. How could they possibly raise enough money? They figured they needed at least $150,000 pledged in a three-year capital campaign from sixty-seven pledge units. At a joint meeting of the building search committee and the board, the district executive suggested they pass around blank slips of paper and each write a number signifying the amount of money they might be willing to pledge in a three-year capital campaign. The district executive made clear that this didn't count—the canvass teams would have to approach them again for real. Nine pledge units responded on those little slips of paper with total projected pledges of $49,000. A third of the goal was already "promised." There were no more questions about whether they could afford it. They went on with the capital campaign and raised $187,000. Today they are in the new building and their membership has nearly doubled.

What are the obstacles to empowerment? One way we stop ourselves is by not believing in ourselves. Or we insist that everything be known before we are willing to begin. Or we talk the subject to death without digging into the details enough to open up the possibilities. Often we block ourselves in the very ways we interact with each other in community.

The best way for us as leaders to meet our needs is to find ways to meet the needs of the volunteers we work with. When we are working for the church, no matter what the task or project, ministry to each other comes first.

~

Roger W. Comstock has twelve years of experience as a District Executive for the Mid-South and Thomas Jefferson Districts. In July 1997 he moved to Charlotte, North Carolina, to devote full-time service to the Thomas Jefferson District.

Generational Diversity in Our Churches

Eunice Milton Benton

On a Sunday in April 1994, a small group gathered to explore forming a new Unitarian Universalist congregation in Oxford, Mississippi. About fifteen people formed a circle around the facilitator. Among their many hopes and dreams, one wish dominated all the others: that the new congregation would affirm and connect members of all generations.

Some in the circle had grown up in close-knit churches. They could remember how the older members of the congregations had been models and mentors for them and had contributed to their developing lives. These founding members wished that same thing for their children. The desire that this congregation be a community of many generations was unanimously affirmed. As the group has grown and established patterns and structures, that goal has remained one of its undergirding principles.

A church community that hums with the energy of many generations is alive and vital. The Oxford congregation began by affirming and celebrating the value of young and old together. Not all congregations begin with such a vision, and many aren't able to keep people of many generations among their active membership. One-generational churches often find that a single generation can't sustain themselves for long.

People of all ages and generations yearn to feel that they belong and are understood in a church family. Indeed, the need to be understood and to belong are two of the main reasons people come to church. A church's philosophy and its programming must accommodate these basic yearnings. A sense of belonging is an essential of life; it nourishes a connection to humanity and other living things. Making young and old feel a part of the church is crucial to a church family's health.

A church family needs to proclaim in the way it behaves that there is a place for everyone. If there's no place within a congregation for young people, no peer group with which they can relate, then it's no surprise when none wish to join the church. A church accomplishes a great deal when it manages to provide a sense of belonging to all its members—children, adults, young people, and the elderly.

A minister from another faith visiting my congregation in Winston-Salem, North Carolina, told us about an elderly woman who regularly attended his Sunday morning worship, even though she was lame, nearly blind, and so deaf that she probably couldn't hear the music or the words of worship. "Miss Ellie," he had asked loudly as he took her hand one Sunday morning, "why do you come to church these days?" Miss Ellie responded, "To be touched."

For people searching for a church, an accepting community is fundamental. Many experts predict that in the coming decades people of all ages will evaluate prospective church homes according to whether they feel valued and connected to others. More than the location of the church, its prestige, or family habit and tradition, this need to be connected and supported by a community can influence the coming generation's choice of a prospective church. Both the individuals and the community, undergirded and empowered by such support, are energized and thus are more able to reach out to the larger world. Creating a healthy and supportive community within the church may be the church's most important mission.

Our church families are sometimes upset by generational differences. The once-charming little girl suddenly appears with pierced body parts and orange hair. The young man we remember as a small shepherd in the holiday pageant now asks for changes in the Sunday morning order of service—a service that has gone unchanged for a decade.

What's a congregation to do? How do we address these differences when they cause conflict? How do we keep them from dividing our church families?

The Winston-Salem congregation used the town meeting format to resolve this sort of conflict. In the late 1980s they discovered that some newcomers wanted a different format for Sunday morning services. For as long as anyone could remember the service had ended with a talk-back, when the speaker of the morning took questions from the congregation and a discussion around the topic of the morning ensued. People often got up and filled their coffee cups and continued the discussion. They enjoyed the intellectual stimulation and the opportunity, as one long-term member put it, "to argue with the 'minister'!" This routine had evolved during the early humanist years of the fellowship, when there was no minister, and the pulpit was filled by a progression of speakers from around the community, especially academics. This formula had worked for years.

But now new members wanted a more spiritual tone. And the new minister had specific ideas about the order of service. As the topic was discussed over many weeks, it became clear that there was real conflict around this issue. A new generation of Unitarian Universalists were now members—and their ideas were different from those of the founders who had established and nurtured the fellowship through the fifties and sixties.

At first the worship committee proposed a change in line with the wishes of the minister. Suddenly there were rumblings from long-term members. A particularly unhappy member complained to the board, saying his whole reason for choosing this faith was that he didn't have to listen to a "preacher." But the minister held her ground. She explained that she wanted to provide closure to a worship service in a way other than the discussion. The voices on both sides of the issue grew noisier and more competitive, and no clear resolution was in sight.

In an attempt to give all voices the chance to be heard, the president and the board announced that a town meeting discussion would be held on Sunday night. The group would not vote, but all who wished to speak or listen would have an opportunity to do so. A moderator would facilitate the discussion. Members of the worship committee and the board would be there and would find a solution later.

A compromise evolved. Some Sunday formats would include "reflection and response" at the end of the service, and others would end with a benediction led by the minister. The congregation grew and two new services were implemented. For a while, one of those services ended with the reflection and response and the other with a benediction. Ultimately, the process proved to be successful in leading the congregation from an old established pattern to a new one. Members voiced their differing wishes and concerns. The worship committee and board felt more informed as they worked out the plan. The town meeting had been an enlightening and healing tool.

Communication and understanding are pivotal in resolving conflict. Listening to the stories of others not only is a good use of time, it also is affirming and life-giving. Listening reassures individuals that someone is genuinely interested in them and gives them the sense that they are understood. Churches need to find some structures for airing the voices of the various generations in church families.

All religious communities are affected by generational differences, but in nonauthoritarian Unitarian Universalist communities, generational differences can be striking, even historic. Take the Transcendentalists of the mid-nineteenth century and their conflicts with traditional Unitarian Christians. And in the mid-twentieth century the Humanist movement challenged both Unitarianism and Universalism. Now, in the last decades of the century, another generation is asking for opportunities to talk about God and the Goddess, to explore Eastern and earth-centered rituals and beliefs.

In the middle years of this century, the mainstream of Unitarian Universalist membership was made up of people who had lived through the depression and two world wars. Their nineteenth-century belief in the eternal progress of humanity and the betterment of life—a belief that had undergirded their God-fearing forefathers—had been shattered by depression and wars. Now they turned their affection to the everyday doings of real people rather than a remote God, and they put their faith only in what science could prove to them. Unitarian churches, always open to new ideas, attracted many in this era who rejected the more traditional religious communities and celebrated this open-minded church which allowed them their humanist views.

For many of these folks, the rejection of ritual and of a hierarchical theology, as well as of hellfire-and-brimstone preaching, were at the heart of their reason for joining this religion. They wanted to avoid the unprovable, mushy, ritual-based habits they remembered from their earlier church experiences. But the children of this generation, the baby boomers, are two generations removed from late-nineteenth-century beliefs and never knew the depression or the wars. They are looking for some spiritual food.

In attempting to soothe generational differences, church communities need to understand and affirm that these differences are normal, even to be expected. Churches also should value and acknowledge the contributions and stories of the various generations in its membership. As we do this, we honor the contributions of previous generations as well as the presence of new ones.

A panel format is a good model for sharing stories. One nonreligious yet not-for-profit organization, the Panel of American Women, developed such a format with the goal of creating empathy and understanding between people of different ethnic and religious backgrounds. The Panel had as its operational mission the presentation of panel-based programs to local groups. For each program, the panel of women included a Jew, a Catholic, an African American, a WASP, and a moderator. Each of the women spoke of their own experiences. The audience asked questions and offered comments. A very interesting dialogue usually followed. The format, open and nonconfrontational, involved both the presenters and the audience.

Consider creating a "Panel of Generations" for church programs. Representatives of different generations could tell their own stories about their religious journeys. They could describe the people and events that have influenced their beliefs, their quests to test their beliefs, their reasons for wanting to belong to this congregation, and the rituals that mean most to them. Like the many programs used by lay-led fellowships over the last several decades, in which members told "why I am a Unitarian," this format would be an intergenerational presentation along a similar theme. A facilitator or moderator would probably be needed. The audience would have the opportunity for questions or comments. In such a format, with no views regarded as right or wrong, such sharing could create the kind of understanding that is needed in the multigenerational church family.

~

Eunice Milton Benton is a native southerner who has been an active Unitarian Universalist and a member of the Winston-Salem, North Carolina, congregation for most of her adult life. She recently completed a master's program for which she wrote a thesis about the turn-of-the-century school at Shelter Neck, North Carolina. She is the District Executive for the Mid-South District.

Unitarios Universalistas de Habla Hispana

Ervin Barrios

When I first arrived in the United States, I was shocked to see how unwelcome Mexicans and Latinos were in California, despite the fact that California once had been a Mexican territory. I experienced discrimination firsthand and I saw many other instances of discrimination toward Mexican people, coming from Mexican Americans as well as from white people. I soon realized that those prejudiced against and stereotyping my people thought that all Mexicans are ignorant. What people don't understand is that most Mexican immigrants, including me, have serious problems mastering the English language. If you can overcome this barrier, sometimes you are treated at least differently or even better.

I first heard of Unitarianism through a couple of friends that I had met in 1985. They insisted on inviting me to their church, the First Unitarian Church of San Jose, because they figured I would like what it had to offer. My father was a Presbyterian minister in Mexico City. I had divorced myself from everything that had to do with religion and churches because I was tired of dogmas and imposed restrictions. At first I declined every invitation from my friends in the most polite manner. However, they insisted so much that I said I would go with them only if they would not bother me again.

Although I liked the service, I was discouraged by the cold reception from the people at the church. Nobody talked to me except my friends. I later found out that the church was going through some rough times. My friends did not invite me to church again. When a new minister arrived in February 1986, they told me some interesting things about her. Intrigued, I came back to hear her speak at a Sunday service. That's how I met the Reverend Lindi Ramsden, who showed a great deal of interest in talking to me after the service. She invited me to lunch that same week.

After lunch, we talked for a while and I was drawn to participate in the church's social concerns committee. This committee was organizing a series of presentations to raise awareness about United States foreign policies in Central America, and to advocate for the church's becoming a sanctuary for Salvadoran refugees. I was invited to be an interpreter for one of the witnesses of the war. This was not an easy task for me. I had been living in the United States for only a year and a half, and I was quite nervous about speaking English in front of a crowd. However, everything went well, and after the presentations the members of the First Unitarian Church of San Jose voted unanimously to become a sanctuary church for Salvadoran refugees.

The church invited a few refugees to live with some of the congregation's members. These people stayed with us for a year, and additional refugees came for a second year. One of the refugees became the sexton for our church. Our church also offered space for a Salvadoran refugee office and Comite Ellacuría para Refugiados de Centro America (CERCA) was born. We saw a great number of Central Americans come and go through our church building. During this time, these visitors asked questions: Who are the Unitarian Universalists? What kind of a church is this and what do you believe?

The Reverend Lindi Ramsden interacted with many of the CERCA members. She was able to explain the principles of Unitarian Universalism, but nonetheless they wanted to know why the church didn't offer worship services in Spanish. Her answer was simple: "Because I don't speak good Spanish." "Well," they said, "you have some bilingual people in your church. You could start something with them." The next thing I knew, I was sitting in a meeting with some CERCA people and several bilingual people from the church. The purpose for our meeting was to consider the possibility of starting an outreach ministry for Spanish-speaking people. This program would be an extension of the existing congregation.

When I first had come to the congregation, it was composed mostly of white, middle-class people, with only two or three people of different ethnic backgrounds. The church was located in the middle of a Latino immigrant neighborhood. I thought that it was the perfect ground to start working toward diversity and plurality.

I and another church member, Oscar Nuñez, went to Boston to attend a training at the Unitarian Universalist Association on how to start new congregations. By the time Oscar and I came back to San Jose, we had a tentative work plan. We invited church members to hear, discuss, and participate in our plan. To my surprise, we received a good turnout and a very positive response.

We were aware of the challenges of this outreach project. No Unitarian Universalist materials were written in Spanish. We needed to translate sermons, poems, readings, songs, prayers, and other liturgical elements from English to Spanish, or we had to find suitable materials originally written in Spanish. The complexity of the task was tremendous, and we knew we needed to be together in every step of the project's development. However, we had a great advantage: we possessed all the infrastructure of the First Unitarian Church of San Jose.

First we translated some of the church's informational material and sent it to the Spanish-speaking community in our area. Next we prepared our first worship service in Spanish. We also asked other congregations for any leads in finding either original or translated liturgical materials or publications about Unitarian Universalism. We received an encouraging letter from Mr. Jaime de Marcos from Barcelona, Spain, who was producing a Unitarian newsletter. He sent us a couple of issues and gave us the very few leads he had about Unitarian material published in Spanish (nothing officially Unitarian Universalist). In the meantime we decided to write grant proposals in order to hire a part-time coordinator for our outreach program.

Our first worship service in Spanish happened in December 1993. We had translated Ramsden's sermon into Spanish, and then we sat with her to go through the correct pronunciation. We were all excited and nervous at the same time. We had a very nice group of people, including many English-speaking members who decided to share this experience with us and to support our service.

Some of our English-speaking musicians gladly participate in Spanish-speaking services by sharing their talents. Other people try to create a bridge of communication by going to school to learn Spanish, or by joining us in social and cultural activities. Little by little, we all are coming to know each other beyond our food and our music. We are helping each other to break the old stereotypes, to worship together, and to work together in the struggle for justice.

The most time-consuming part of putting together a Spanish worship service is the translation work. We created a team of people who are qualified translators and are interested in rotating such a task. Once the sermon is translated we do a final editing, and many times we work with our speaker to refine the pronunciation and phonetics. One of our major challenges in performing a service is trying to keep the flow of the service as natural as possible. The spontaneity of observations and comments in the sermon and other elements of the liturgy are significantly reduced when the speaker has to follow the text at the risk of using improper expressions.

Translating songs is not an easy task either. It is like translating poetry, which loses its rhyming scheme in translation, and English words that had fit a specific musical meter don't fit in Spanish. We therefore look for Latin-American songs that convey a message related to Unitarian Universalist values. To our surprise we have found many of them. To this day we have gathered about thirty-five songs, including ones that have been translated from English to Spanish. Some of these songs can be played by piano or organ if we happen to come across printed music, but most are played by a guitar, bass, and drums, or they are performed "a capella." We also have Andean music and instruments. Our music brings a new dimension to the service, and in a certain way it reminds us of the liberation theology services in Latin America. Most of the members and friends who attend our Spanish services come from a Catholic background, and they are not used to active participation in a worship service. This has been a challenge for our newer members, and although many of them are willing to do it, standing in front of a group is the first fear for them to overcome.

Sometimes when the whole church gathers to worship together, our services are bilingual. Most English speakers in our congregation are getting used to reading Spanish through songs and affirmations. Our challenge is to make the service flow as smoothly as possible, so that not all the concepts are being said or repeated in English and Spanish, which could double the length of the service.

Several churches in California are considering the possibility of starting a ministry similar to ours. Except for the First Unitarian Church in Los Angeles, which has a Spanish-speaking group working on their own without a Spanish-speaking minister, very few other Unitarian Universalist churches are reaching out to the Latino community. Most of the Unitarian Universalist churches along the US border with Mexico have the potential to succeed if they are willing to do so.

Several congregations are showing interest in our church's Spanish worship materials. We have received requests from other Unitarian Universalist congregations in the US, as well as from people in Argentina and Mexico. What started as a small attempt to reach out to Spanish-speaking people soon will be demanding the attention of the offices of the Unitarian Universalist Association.

Other Latinos in our Association around the continental US have triggered the creation of Latino Unitarian Universalist National Association (LUUNA). LUUNA shows that Latinos of all walks of life are highly interested in Unitarian Universalist principles and values. Our hope is that one day we will see the development of an international Spanish-speaking Unitarian Universalist movement.

The pioneering phase for an outreach program like ours is unique in many ways. Although we started this ministry within the infrastructure of an existing church, we were working at a missionary level. In order to attract an ethnic community that had never heard of Unitarian Universalism and did not have many reading materials or information available to them, we had to offer services and activities that were sponsored by people who did not belong to the community we wanted to serve. This was difficult because in order to make our outreach program work, we needed to attract a critical mass of people who would make Unitarian Universalism an important part of their lives, important enough for them to invest their finances in our ministry. We could not expect this to happen until we could provide all the assistance that any other congregation would offer.

Those of us who are working in this ministry are learning in the process, but we know that we do not yet have all the necessary elements. Although we are already attracting a considerable number of Latinos (some of them already pledging to our church), we feel that there is more to a congregation than just having worship services. We have yet to tailor many elements to the specific needs and views of a Latino culture. It is not just a matter of translating materials from the English language. We need to have sufficient cultural understanding to eliminate the language barriers. Unfortunately, we still have very few Spanish-speaking Unitarian Universalist ministers. However, there are at least three Latino ministers, and others are studying for the Unitarian Universalist ministry, so there is hope.

When I look at the Catholic and Protestant churches in San Jose who offer worship services in Spanish, and I see the number of people who are attending their services, I realize that Latino people in the United States have a great spiritual interest. I also know that many Latino people would prefer Unitarian Universalist values to their traditional Catholic, Protestant, and other religious values if they only had the opportunity to find out about our church. That's why I think we have a missionary ministry—Latino people are just starting to discover who we are.

~

Ervin Barrios was born in the state of Chiapas, Mexico, and grew up in Mexico City, where he studied architecture and languages. He now works as a Spanish translator in San Jose, California.

Our Ministry to Children

Susan Davison Archer

I once knew a girl I'll call Anna. I'd known her for several years the night I discovered her sitting in the dark sanctuary after an intergenerational Christmas service. She was alone on the platform, looking quite small next to the tall, broad fir tree that was the focus of the service. The other children and adults had moved to a room nearby, where we could hear conversation and laughter—the sounds of a holiday potluck supper.

Anna's parents were in the midst of a difficult divorce, and recently Anna's life had been unpredictable. Usually Anna would be first in line, but on this particular night she sat alone in this empty, half-dark room.

We all know what it is like to have to sort out a life-shaking event, something that we will later use to measure "before" and "after." Unfortunately, children are not spared such experiences. For Anna, the imminent divorce was the collapse of what she had understood as familiar. She was emotionally exhausted moving from "before" to "after." She needed some time, and space, in between.

Most of us experience transitions as significant, and children are no exception. Because of the rapid succession of their developmental stages and because they have less control than adults over their external circumstances, children are often in the midst of major change. It is especially during these "in-between" times that our ministry to children can make a deep and lasting impact.

As a child one of my favorite verses was A. A. Milne's poem "Halfway Down," which tells what it's like when "I'm not at the bottom, / I'm not at the top." I loved nooks and crannies—the landing, the turn in the hallway, places without a lot of definition. Cozy places. Places where it wasn't always clear which direction I might go. They were places for thinking, for sorting things out. They were not always comfortable places, but they were important.

For Anna this safe place did not simply emerge magically on Christmas Eve. She was able to find it because she had been nurtured in our religious community over the years. This was a place where people ministered to her, giving her the gift of belonging. On this holiday night Anna could be sure that this was a place where people would pay attention to her needs, where she could be safely in between. Not surprisingly, a couple of adults who knew Anna noticed her there. They simply stood nearby, and at one point they whispered new directions to the custodian who came to close up the sanctuary. After a while one of them approached Anna and gently asked if she was ready for dinner. She was.

Children need ministry. Sometimes this may be a simple matter of protecting a quiet moment of safety. Anna's pain was uniquely her own, but the fact of the pain is not at all unique. Often at children's worship, I've listened to painful stories—lost friendships, dying relatives, unrealized dreams. The list of troubles is not very different from what adults experience. Like adults, children need to be listened to, they need to be valued, they need a community that will always be there. And sometimes they simply need a quiet place to sit.

Our gurus of human development and faith stages tell us that these in-between places are some of the hardest, and the most creative. For children these places come often and in rapid succession. No sooner do they reach one developmental destination than they are on the move again, up or down the stairs, into or out of a stage. And each time a child returns to the landing, she is both the same person and also different. Each time she returns, there is the potential for her to have become stronger and more complex. There is also the danger that she will be overwhelmed and exhausted. Caring adults can make all the difference.

Less quiet and solitary are the predictable stresses and joys of normal development. Some striking examples come from our teenagers, who can experience especially hard or confusing times. Parents often say: "He's going through a stage!"

Our youth group has a long tradition of keeping an ongoing "housebook" to record their ideas and feelings.

Over the years many volumes of this book have marked the comings and goings of young people, many of whom are by now old enough to be parents of their own teenagers! One of those groups gave me permission to read and quote from their writings. Here is a passage written by a young woman of fourteen.

Before.
Before the change occurred.
When life was sweet and simple
And laughter was the only language.

Then.
Then the change occurred.
It left me all alone
In a big hole of blackness.
It took control of me,
And left me in a land unknown.

Now.
Now the change has occurred.
I've crossed the bridge.
And I shall never return.
It's taken me,
And left me with just memories.
Of before.

We should not underestimate the difficulties of such transitions. Teens need to know what adults think, to see what we are committed to and how we live out our commitments. Our role is to be part of an unchanging, ever-present faith group for these young people. Teens need our affirmation as they experiment with different identities, seek to understand their sexual orientation, and work through the moral and personal aspects of relationship and justice issues. We must never believe that they don't need us and want us. When they need to step back from their parents, other caring adults are very important.

Three years later, the same young woman, now seventeen, was about to move away, and wrote this in the housebook:

This is the End.
This is the Beginning.
If Life goes in cycles—
I've completed one period.
I want to thank the people in the UU community
for all your love and support . . .
To help me discover Who I am and
What I aspire to.
Thank you for accepting me and making me feel
comfortable with all of me.
I love you guys!
High school would have never been the same without your influence!
Everything is ephemeral,
So live, live and never regret.
Carpe Diem.

The world is awaiting for you.
Love and Peace.

Sitting on a stair, halfway down, a person can decide to go in either direction. One of the gifts we can give our kids is the chance to practice seeing issues from more than one side. Church can be a place for sitting on a stair in between, without needing to end inner dissonance too quickly. Our religious community can be a touchstone as we stretch ourselves to understand ambiguous questions, to tolerate other points of view.

We need to be nurturing children who will not look for an easy fix to their own problems or those of the world. It is ministry when we raise children who have a growing tolerance for ambiguity, children who can appreciate open minds and critical debate. We in liberal religious communities are in a unique position to hold one another in the uncomfortable place of being unsure. We are in a unique position to support the growth of children who can find strength in the face of the complex problems of the twenty-first century.

How do we do this? We know that as children grow there are particular times when we, as a religious community, can help them develop open minds. For a start, we can reinforce a powerful sense of self-esteem and belonging, from the first moment that child walks or is carried through our doors. Beginning about first grade, we can help them explore what it's like to stand in another's shoes. It is ministry when we help them talk with each other about their feelings and needs, ministry when we model ways of respecting the feelings and needs of others and ourselves.

Around the age of eight or nine, children itch to demonstrate their competence. They love to identify a problem and find a way to fix it. They have discovered that they can make things happen! They want to be participants and partners. Our religious communities are fertile grounds for letting them try out their skills. It is ministry when we invite children to participate in doing the real tasks of the community, when we acknowledge their competence. It is ministry when we work together—we fold newsletters, clean up the building, rake the leaves, serve food to the homeless. It is ministry when we encourage, when we notice, and when we appreciate the projects they organize on their own.

Between eleven and thirteen years of age, kids begin to make giant steps in the ability to think critically, to deal with ambiguity. They start the lifelong struggle to figure out not simply what's right but also how to choose between two conflicting values, between two "rights."

Several years ago, a sixth-grade religious education class was given permission to create signs for the congregation's Wayside Pulpit. In the weeks that passed since permission was given, Kuwait was invaded and US military forces deployed. The class's first Wayside Pulpit message read: "Bring 'em back—From Iraq!" The brand new sign was prominently displayed at the front of the building as adults streamed out of Sunday morning worship.

Complaints began less than twenty minutes after close of class that day. "Not only does their sign not represent me," said one angry adult, "but it is not even accurate! Our troops aren't in Iraq! In any event, no sentiment that represents a view that we as a congregation are not clear nor mostly unified about should be put in a public place!" He had a point. The sign was temporarily removed (replaced with a message about the rainforest, also by the class) until some way of mediating this issue could be worked out. The next Sunday the class was asked to respond.

One student presented the problem: "If we believe in peace (one of our principles, see it hanging on our classroom wall!), but we also believe in democratic process (also a principle on the wall), what do we do when not everyone agrees on how peace comes or what makes a lasting peace? Some members felt hurt and excluded by our sign. But some of us feel very strongly that US policy must be changed! Should we be allowed to express our view and work for peace in our way?"

These children were ardently dedicated to peace. Their teachers, who over time had earned their trust, gently pushed them to think about how others equally committed to peace might think differently about how that commitment should be lived out in this situation. "Oh." Some inner light came on. Some kids began to agree with complainants. Others held fast to all the reasons the sign needed to be displayed in the first place. They went back and forth. Some children changed their minds several times as multiple considerations were brought up.

Where did ministry come in? It came with the time, care, depth, and patience of the adult leaders as they engaged these young people in conversation about a difficult and important issue. The trusted adults in that room helped those children learn how to honor complexity and how to sit in that uncomfortable place "in between" where answers are not sure. By the end of the discussion, a few young people were thinking about possible justification for engaging our troops in the Middle East. Most stayed committed to no military force at all. But all of them were committed to hearing and respecting multiple points of view.

They decided it was inappropriate—without a vote of the congregation—to put up their Wayside Pulpit sign. They asked the board of trustees for permission to establish a "World Issues Opinion Board" where their views, and the views of others, could always be expressed. The board approved, delighted with their process and their request. In fact, these children set the tone for further conversation about the war among the adults in the congregation.

The tolerance that allows us to sit on the step halfway in between does not excuse us from making moral judgments. But it does require that we draw upon all the experience, knowledge, compassion, and understanding that we have, to acknowledge the complexities involved, and then to act for what we reasonably discern as most right for us all. We learn to do this by being encouraged to do it, by being part of a community that regularly challenges itself, one that is willing to sit on the step for a while, before climbing up or down.

The Unitarian Universalist understanding of a religious person is one who doesn't cling to feelings and ideas that are comfortable, doesn't insist on easy, quick answers, doesn't hide from complexity. In this religious community of the faithful, we must nurture our capacity to sit with the uncomfortable, on the step halfway down, until that inner guide lets us move to the next place. Our ministry calls us to make sure we include our children, especially those preadolescents and teens who are ready to be critical thinkers. This ministry cannot happen, however, unless we find institutional roles that let us know and to be with our kids. What are these roles?

Be a class leader. Be a youth group advisor. Be a special friend (in a congregation-wide program that connects individual children to specific adults). Be a mentor in a coming-of-age program. Be a caregiver (by including children on the lists given to the caring committee, or create a caring committee that focuses specifically on children and youth). Be a classroom aide to a child with special needs.

More generally, there are roles we can take on in all aspects of life in our religious communities:

Engage with children when you encounter them. Speak to them in the hall, admire their handicrafts, ask for their opinions! Most of all, really listen.

Include them—in worship, in social action projects, in the celebration of birth, in the mourning of death, in your newsletter, in the marches to legislatures, in the petitions to Congress, in the exhibitions of arts, in yoga class. There are, of course, times for children to be engaged primarily with other children and adults with adults. But many times they can be given an invitation in the same manner as everyone else in the congregation.

Be an advocate for them. Look for ways to make children a more integrated part of the community. Probably the most important reason for this connection is that it provides an opportunity to be "at home" in our religious community. In difficult times, as with Anna and many of our adolescents, there will be times when church may be more home than home.

Empower them! Admire their competence and use their skills. Don't just ask them to wash dishes after the potluck (you'd be amazed at the number of committees who ask them this!). Also ask them, as it is age appropriate, to serve on committees, to lead worship, to give input to congregational decisions. Let them know how they can initiate their own projects if they so choose, how to reserve a date on the congregation's calendar, even how to get permission to use the copier.

Delight in them! They find their own inner light by noticing the dancing light that they can inspire in your eyes. Don't hold back! You may find places of laughter and wonder you had forgotten!

All these roles count in our ministry to our kids. When we are doing it right, we are helping them grow a sense of self that will last a lifetime and will make a difference that is bigger than one person.

What we do with our children in RE and in the faith community is not simply nice stuff for kids. It is crucial! Our children come to understand and live their faith by being in communities with worthy adults who are living the principles of our faith and who are loving the children. It is a dynamite combination.

We cannot underestimate the tremendous responsibility of being adults in our religious communities. When we enter our children's lives, especially at those moments halfway down and halfway up, we may make all the difference.

~

Susan Davison Archer is a Minister of Religious Education currently serving as District Religious Education Consultant for the District of Metropolitan New York. She is the mother of three teenagers and formerly served as the Religious Educator at the First Unitarian Church of Monmouth, New Jersey.

The Call and Joy of Young Adult Ministry

Shelby Greiner

Unitarian Universalism is not just about Sunday morning services, committee meetings, or agendas. It is a way of embracing the world and moving through life by making the most of our daily opportunities to touch the lives of people around us. No interaction is without its impact and every act of respect, no matter how small, is an act of revolution and social justice.

Ministry exists in all that we do. One meaning of the word "minister" is "agent." As a lay minister I am an agent of social justice, of change, of my religious beliefs. Most of all, I am called to serve as an agent of something greater than myself. By recognizing myself as part of a greater whole, I honor all the people who have given of themselves to me throughout my life. Every interaction between people holds the opportunity for ministry, and I pass on the inheritance of love I have received so that it may bless the larger world.

When I look back over my life as a Unitarian Universalist, I see that my experiences as a young adult are responsible for my deep passion for this religion. One of the most crucial changes from youth to young adulthood is the transformation from being "ministered to" to ministering to others. As a young adult, one ministers to oneself and one's peers. As one finds a home of one's own choosing within the Unitarian Universalist community, one can minister to others. As a youth I took. I received gifts of energy, time, and resources from my home church that far outweighed any contributions I made. My contributions were largely unconscious or the result of a special occasion, such as helping with a rummage sale or holding a bake sale to fund a church project. Mostly I consumed and received, I was mentored and nurtured, and I was unconscious of the disparity.

Growing up in the Unitarian Universalist church community, I was heavily involved in Young Religious Unitarian Universalist (YRUU) activities. There I learned a vision of community that has sustained me since. Youth are ministered to by their parents, youth advisors, and ideally the minister and the wider Unitarian Universalist community. It is appropriate to be fed and nurtured in these crucial years of personal development, to receive the space to explore and discover and create while still within the protective and supportive walls of the parental community.

However, our generosity to youth also carries the promise to honor the people they are. It is hypocritical to tell youth what wonderful, powerful, and amazing people they are, and then fail to create a real way for them to connect to the church as adults.

After I had graduated from high school, I found nothing else in Unitarian Universalism that matched the depth, connectedness, and spontaneous joy of my youth community. At that time no young adult-focused ministry or activities existed in my part of the continent. My friends and I decided to change that. I became an activist, working hard to override the view that it was a waste of time and resources to appeal to recently graduated youth or young adults because they wouldn't stay around.

I joined the fledgling young adult ministry movement because I felt a tremendous desire to serve my church community. The investment my church had made in me as a youth became the fuel that powered my energetic development as a lay minister. This harvest of love and energy has tremendous implications for Unitarian Universalism, if we can understand the need to channel it into productive and self-realized expression.

Until the last few years, very little has been done on an institutional level to meet the ministry needs of this age population (eighteen to thirty-five years). We have done for ourselves a kind of peer ministry, learning from each other as we go along and discovering power in ourselves and in the community we could create. Many of us grew up in Unitarian Universalist churches and have had the incredible intimacy of our Liberal Religious Youth and YRUU experiences to draw on.

Many young adults go from their young adult communities into theological school, perhaps thinking that attending theological school is the only way a young adult can deepen his or her faith. I offer lay ministry as an alternate route, a way to feed one's soul and spiritual appetite. For a while I was tempted by the idea of studying professional ministry. There is a certain romance about professional clergy (I hear the professional clergy laughing out there, but it is true). They have a tight professional community. They are encouraged to develop themselves, to discover their inner gifts, and to speak clearly with their own voice. I think we all crave on some level to discover our own voice and vision and to have that celebrated.

I find lay ministry is a path with a huge range of possibilities. You can develop whichever skills you find most attractive. You can practice it wherever you wish (as opposed to wherever you can find a job). You can devote as much or as little time to it as you wish. You can work with senior high youth, preschoolers, the auction committee, the social concerns committee, or the worship committee.

I bring my skills and my Unitarian Universalist worldview to everything that I do. I practice the majority of my lay ministry at work where I try to live out my Unitarian Universalist values as actively as I can without mentioning my religious affiliation to my coworkers. Until very recently, I worked for an academic department at a large university, a place concerned with rank and ranking, with title and degree and seniority. In small daily ways, I put to use the values that my church community taught me. My office was warm and decorated with bright colors and inviting posters. I kept a small army of wind-up toys on my desk and put cartoons on the door. People came to regard my office as a place to stop, even for just a minute or two, and find something to make them smile.

Young adults bring to lay ministry a willingness to play, engage, take risks, and make mistakes, and to respect individual boundaries as important parts of community. We come as we are to the circle and we create a place of acceptance and love. We explore each other and ourselves and share our discoveries. I've watched my friends examine their pride and prejudices, stepping into other viewpoints to see what the world looks like from over there. We rejoice in the opportunity to stretch our perceptions of who we are and what we can do. We've sought social justice within Unitarian Universalism for all people who call it home, an equity that embraces the whole without losing sight of the individual. We bring conscious attention to all aspects of our lives, weaving worship, play, work, and friendship into a pleasantly whole fabric.

I remember sitting in a Sunday morning worship service at our district's annual meeting a few years back with my friends Laura and Mark. Laura and I had grown up together in YRUU and have been loving friends for more than sixteen years. Mark was just eighteen at the time. I had known him as a youth and had encouraged him to join our district young adult community when he came of age. We sang the hymn "For All That Is Our Life," which I had not heard before, and it filled me with such joy that I choked. To be standing there, holding Mark's hand and embracing Laura with my other arm, to be in my beloved church community, and to see my involvement stretch out on either side of me to encompass my entire life—I cried with the utter joy of that vision. And I saw that all I had been given as a child and youth in church was now blossoming within me. From that fullness I was being called to return these gifts, magnified by my own experiences, to this community. Gratitude and joy and love welled up within me, filling me and spilling out to embrace the whole hall in a flood of bright, self-giving love.

That epiphany showed me a deep well within myself of passion, experience, and love that I can touch and draw on. Since then, at conferences and in meetings, at 10:00 a.m. on Sunday mornings and at 2:00 a.m. on Friday nights, I have discovered that many of my young adult friends also have this place of passion within themselves and are similarly moved to build the common good and make their own days glad. To me, this is the core vision of young adult ministry and the greatest joy in my life.

~

Shelby Greiner, aka Sheba, currently resides in Seattle, Washington, and is a member of the Edmonds Unitarian Universalist Church. Since her involvement in YRUU as a teenager, she has served in many leadership roles on the continental level and is one of the original authors of the Bridging Ceremony.

Creating the Intergenerational Community

Cindy Spring

At a recent district gathering for directors of religious education (DREs), we asked an old question: How do we bring the church community together? In my role as district religious education consultant, I often witness the tensions that arise when the RE program is seen as a separate part of the congregation. Perhaps the parish minister is in charge of the adult program, and the DRE is in charge of the children and youth. I hear "yours" and "mine" instead of "ours."

At the district meeting, a new DRE talked about the separation she experienced between the children's program and the adults. She knew that the church community would be harmed if this separation were allowed to continue. The discussion was lively; this is an old and troubling problem. A lot is at stake and there is no quick fix.

Most Unitarian Universalist buildings are planned for good programming. There is a space for adult worship, another for coffee hour and potluck suppers, and a third for meetings and adult discussion groups. There are offices for the staff and rooms for the church school. Sometimes there is a special place for the children to worship. Separate spaces are necessary because different age groups have different needs. Children need space to move, and adults don't fit comfortably in little chairs.

But sometimes children and adults are separated needlessly. There may be a separation between the "adult" church and the "children's" church, a problem that can become especially apparent when a church builds new spaces. I have heard of churches who are having a separate coffee hour for the church school; even after the morning's activities are over, the community is still separate.

Perhaps the first way to bridge this gap is for the parish minister to spend time with the children and youth and the religious educator to spend time with the adults. The parish minister might attend an occasional youth group meeting, tell the story when the children are in the sanctuary, meet twice a year with the RE committee, spend a morning or two in the church school.

The religious educator can colead some of the adult curricula, give an adult sermon once or twice a year, make a point of attending board meetings, be part of the "Welcoming Congregation" program, and participate in potlucks and other all-church activities. (As a side benefit, she or he then can better assess the pool of potential church school leaders!)

The parish minister and religious educator should be meeting on a regular basis to talk about the congregation they both serve. As they share information and ideas, they help the congregation as a whole understand that all ages are members of one congregation.

Why have an intentionally intergenerational community? The congregation is everyone who comes together on Sunday morning. This includes babies and nintey-five year olds. If you look around the sanctuary and see no one under the age of twenty, you are not seeing "the congregation." And those not seen are easily forgotten. Everyone should be concerned about the lack of space in church school rooms, the lack of teachers, and the poor compensation paid to the religious educator. I have heard of cases when the fourth- or fifth-grade class was sent into the adult service as a way of demonstrating that there was no adult willing to be with them. This is a dramatic example of a way to help the congregation see and own its children. I don't encourage this, because it portrays the children as victims. There are better ways than guilt to get adults to respond.

The children and youth are our future. Our churches were full in the 1950s and 1960s, but only 8 percent of us now were brought up Unitarian Universalist. What happened to all of those youngsters from the fifties and sixties? There are many possible answers, but a clue may be found in my own story. I was raised a Unitarian in St. Paul, Minnesota. We had a lovely building with large classrooms and a private children's chapel. I rode to church with my parents each Sunday, said good-bye at the door, went downstairs, and met up again at coffee hour. Each Christmas we went into the sanctuary for the pageant, in which most of us had roles. That was the only time I can remember being in the "adult" space. I am still a Unitarian Universalist but many of my church school friends are not.

We need our children and youth with us in our church lives to remind us that we are all learning and growing. And they need us. The bright wondering three year old, the careful, considering nine year old, the idealistic sixteen year old—they all should be part of who we are as a religious people. We need to hear their questions and to search with them for the answers. We need to see ourselves through their eyes. At a recent General Assembly I was in a small group with a number of adults and three teens. Near the end, one of the adults who had been particularly hard on the youth said, "I want to thank you for helping me see how jaded I have become."

We can become awfully smug, thinking we have arrived at the truth. There was a discussion of the Unitarian Universalist Principles at a youth conference not long ago, about which ones held concern for the youth. Instead of taking them for granted, as many adults do, they were asked to really think about them. For example, do we believe in the democratic process, even when through voting, a law is passed that denies rights to gay, lesbian, bisexual, and transgendered folks? Do we understand the interconnected web to include ants, mosquitoes, and dandelions? Do we believe in the inherent worth and dignity of those who support the radical right? The principles are wonderful guidelines to help us, but they can and will be changed, perhaps by some of our youth!

Wisdom doesn't reside only in the teenagers. Not long

ago, when the Keene, New Hampshire, church was beginning the search process, the younger children were asked what they thought would be important in a new minister. The church printed their answer in the newsletter: "The minister should be kind, be helpful to people, be willing to listen to everyone—including children, be able to be serious as well as playful, and should not always talk about God in the same way." Children are wise, caring, and open. We can't afford as a religious faith to ignore them.

Our children and youth need to get to know us. Many of us have moved from our hometowns or state and no longer live near our extended families. Our children are growing up without grandparents, aunts, and uncles. They need adults to talk with and learn from who are not grading them, correcting them, or depending on them to further the family's "good name."

Think of the areas of congregational life—worship, education, social action, and community building. Perhaps the most important is worship. How can we learn to worship together? As a child I never experienced intergenerational worship. In many of our societies now the children and youth are present for the first part of the adult worship service, whether once a month or every week. In some of our churches they stay for the opening words and a story, then leave during the first hymn. In others, they are present for the "Candles of Joys and Concern" and are invited to light candles for significant events in their lives. This also gives them a chance to hear the moments of joy or sorrow in the lives of the adult members. It is a rare gift when a child is invited to share a sorrow with an adult.

Many of our congregations celebrate the holidays by holding an all-ages worship service. It's not easy to plan a service that will be meaningful to both five and fifty year olds, but it is worth the challenge. One of the keys is to help the congregation realize that being together as a worshiping community is, in itself, a religious experience. Often these services are best planned jointly by the worship and religious education committees. Children and youth may be brought into the planning, too.

The summer services are all intergenerational at my fellowship. They are small and lay-led, and usually there's a time to respond to the story or reading. It is wonderful to have adults and children listening to each other in a respectful, nonjudging way.

One of the most popular services of the year is the youth-led service. I'm glad that the adults have a chance to really listen to our youth, but I am sorry that the youth are so seldom in the sanctuary to listen to the adults. We still have a long way to go in learning how to worship together.

Education and learning are important activities in congregational life. When I was a child, I got to know the paid religious educator and one teacher per year. (These were obviously dedicated volunteers!) Thanks to team-teaching, our children today become acquainted with many more adults.

Some of our congregations offer "Coming of Age" programs for youth. This often includes a mentoring activity in which a youth and an adult team up and are encouraged to spend time together talking, playing, learning, and getting to know each other. Two teams might meet for a specific activity. Sometimes all the teams come together for a joint meal and discussion. Each youth is encouraged to ask questions such as how the adult lives out his or her faith. This gives adults who are not parents or whose children have grown real contact with youth.

Social action also can provide intergenerational contact. The children's curriculum may encourage kids to choose a project—starting a recycling program, promoting a mitten tree during the holidays, or collecting food once a month for the local pantry. All of these activities include making adults aware of what the children are doing and encouraging them to participate. One can go beyond articles in the newsletter and posters at coffee hour to announcements by children from the pulpit.

In the ideal church, the social action committee finds a way for interested children and youth to be involved in any churchwide project. Perhaps a member from the committee visits the children's chapel or the individual classrooms to tell about the project. Youth groups are often encouraged to work with Habitat for Humanity or with the local soup kitchen, but it can start much sooner. Young children are willing and eager to share with those less fortunate. They need to be shown ways that they can make a difference.

A program for visiting church members who are homebound or in nursing homes is another way to bridge the generation gap. And such visits need not be restricted to Christmas: What if each month a child visited the same adult? By the end of the year they would know each other pretty well. The need to be noticed and appreciated is universal. Let's find ways to meet that need in each other!

Perhaps the easiest intergenerational activity is intentional community building. A popular example is the "special friend" activity. In the past this was often called the *secret* friend program, but as we begin teaching our children about unsafe secrets, we need to be careful about our use of the term. This activity usually calls for an adult drawing the name of a child from the congregation and then sending notes and small gifts for a week or two. In some congregations, each child draws the name of an adult to befriend. Sometimes youth group members "adopt" a younger child. At the end of the specified time, the two "friends" meet during a culmination ceremony. Some special friend programs last for a month or a year; others happen on a single Sunday and are the basis for an intergenerational service. All are worthwhile because they make the adults and the children see one another as individuals. We are all so different, but it is easy to lump members of an age group together and then see their worst side—"all children are noisy and undisciplined," "all youth love loud music," "all adults are self-centered and boring."

Some congregations hold family game nights. Everyone's invited and asked to bring a favorite table game. Candyland may be happening right next to Monopoly or Chutes and Ladders. All ages mingle, and often there's a shared snack halfway through the evening. Or a leader can lead participatory games for all ages. Those who don't want to join in a particular game can sit and watch. These are often more active games, and great for the six to twelve year olds.

Potluck birthday dinners can mix up the generations. Participants sit at tables according to the month of their birthday. They talk about what it is like to have a birthday always in the summer when school is out or always near Halloween or Christmas. As a dessert, each table is given a cake to decorate together. This is a simple way to divide families into new groupings.

When you are having a congregational dinner for all ages, it can help to put a list of questions on each table to be read, answered by each person, and discussed. For example, at a Harvest Dinner each person could be asked, "What did you like best this summer?" or "What are you looking forward to this fall?" Again, this gives each individual a chance to hear and be heard.

In our largest congregations, the event could be held in smaller groupings, perhaps by ZIP code, so that folks of all ages could meet and mingle on a regular basis.

Cakes for the Queen of Heaven, our feminist theology curriculum, has resulted in the tradition of annual mother/daughter dinners. Recently some congregations have held father/son events, another wonderful chance to connect the ages.

One of my own fond memories is summer day camp. About fifty children and youth and fifteen adults were involved. Most of the time we were outside playing and learning together. Each morning started with a short worship we all attended. Then each age group went to its particular spot to begin the day. There were many activities, each led by an adult who had a special interest—nature walks, sun prints, group games, or drama. We could watch other groups doing their thing. One year we all piled into cars to go fossil hunting. On rainy days we might all move inside to watch and discuss a movie or to hear a storyteller.

When I was old enough to serve as one of the helpers, I was thrilled. The camp was for three to twelve year olds, but older children served as group assistants, lifeguards, and supply staff. I remember meeting early on with the adults and other youth to talk about a theme for the summer and possible activities. My ideas were listened to and appreciated. Working with the adults during the week was liberating—sometimes they made mistakes and admitted it. Amazing!

It was good to see adults in blue jeans and T-shirts getting excited about a butterfly or a wildflower, or in bathing suits enjoying the cool water, or just sitting on a step in the sunlight drinking lemonade. I remember a conversation I had with one of them about what happens after we die. Perhaps I am still a Unitarian Universalist because as a youngster I was able to see beyond the adult to the human being. Let's be sure to give our children and youth chances to do the same.

The Nashua, New Hampshire, Unitarian Universalist Church was an intergenerational puzzle. They had built a lovely religious education wing with lots of space, large classrooms with windows that opened, and a wonderful chapel for children's worship. The families came together at Christmas and for RE Sunday in June, but that was it. I'd been DRE there for about two years, and I worried that there was almost no mix between the ages. I talked with the RE Committee about my concern, and we decided to try something new.

We'd heard that the Milford, New Hampshire, church spent a weekend together each year at Ferry Beach, one of our camp and conference centers, so two of our committee members agreed to go check it out. They came back very enthused, so we reserved a weekend, formed a subcommittee, and began selling the congregation on the idea.

It worked! The first year 156 people attended, and by the second year we had over 200. We would arrive on Friday night, often in the rain, find our cabins or bunks, and then go out somewhere for dinner. There would be a formal in-gathering about 7:00 and then an informal game time. I brought lots of jigsaw puzzles because folks can work on them and get to know each other at the same time.

Saturday would be the long day with plenty of time for tie-dying, playing volleyball, building sandcastles, flying kites, and taking long walks on the beach. There were no set age divisions—folks participated in whatever looked interesting to them. I had noticed that at the church, if an adult spoke to a child during coffee hour it was usually to reprimand. At Ferry Beach, the comments were more apt to be positive— "Can I help you with that?" "What a great castle!"

The meals were prepared family-style, and everyone was expected to help. The youngest ones would fold napkins, cut bananas for salad, or count crackers. Teens ran the dishwasher. Mistakes were accepted, and people laughed and learned together.

Saturday night there was a talent show put on by the children and youth. No adult helped in the planning or production, so we were never sure what to expect, but we were never disappointed! The youth became the leaders and did a terrific job of encouraging the younger ones to enjoy being part of the production. If someone got nervous and faltered, someone else helped out. And the adults came in droves to witness the interactions and the various talents of "their" children—the children of their congregation. Many of the adults who came to Ferry Beach were childless. Some were single, others had children living far away. Yet all were there as part of the Nashua Unitarian Universalist family—all felt wanted and needed.

Sunday morning we walked together into the grove for our worship service. There were singing, readings, and a short sermon. Everyone sat on the grass and pine needles. Small children fell asleep in the sunshine. Toddlers played quietly. The natural world around us became an important element in the worship service. After brunch we headed to the beach for a final hour of games before packing and heading home.

Our church lives were subtly changed. People knew each other better, some for the first time. During our second year at Ferry, a fifth-grade boy pointed to a woman in blue jeans. "Is that Mrs. Brown?" he asked. He explained that Mrs. Brown was his piano teacher, but he couldn't imagine her wearing blue jeans. I saw them playing together later that weekend.

If your congregation has never done anything with all ages, start small. Try a week-long special friend program or a family game night. Build on what's already in place. Is there an intergenerational service at Thanksgiving? If so, ask some of the children and youth to take part. Perhaps the younger children could write a responsive reading on what they are thankful for. Maybe a youth could say the opening words or lead the meditation.

Talk with the social action committee about ways that the children and youth could be part of their work. Ask the religious education committee to think about involving more adults who otherwise would not have the opportunity to be with children. Perhaps a member of the youth group could serve on the church board.

Of course things won't go smoothly. Count on it. But the risk is worth it. Our future depends on it.

~

Cindy Spring grew up in Unity Unitarian Church in St. Paul, Minnesota, and later served as Director of Religious Education in Nashua, New Hampshire. She has been the Religious Education Consultant for the New Hampshire/Vermont District since 1988.

~ Serving in the Wider World

Unitarian Universalist Campus Ministry

Margaret L. Beard and Andrea G. Dougherty

The evangelical era appeared at the University of Richmond in the fall of 1990. Religion was a hot issue. Church attendance was up. In the dining hall students could be seen reading the Bible as they ate lunch. Was the Gulf War part of the reason for the widespread interest in fundamentalist Christianity? No one was sure.

For non-Christian students, the increasing evangelism was a problem. Andrea Dougherty was one of these students. Although she was a spiritual person, she didn't consider herself a Christian. Andrea explains:

On campus, I felt pressured to change my beliefs. One of my roommates started leaving biblical tracts on my pillow. I overheard her talking with other Christian friends about how they could get me to "see the light." In spite of all this, I knew myself to be spiritual and I yearned for a religious connection. But I wanted support and an environment that would let me explore and question without judgment.

163

That fall, Andrea and some of her friends visited the First Unitarian Church of Richmond, Virginia, where Margaret Beard was president. As part of a women's studies class assignment, they made an appointment with her to discuss the role of women in the Unitarian Universalist church today. Margaret elaborates:

I thought the purpose of our first meeting was to discuss Unitarian Universalism and the role of women in our church. We went way beyond the information needed for their class paper. When I heard what was happening on campus I knew the church had to do something. We had to help them start a Unitarian Universalist campus ministry. Soon Andrea and several friends were meeting weekly on campus, and my husband Rick and I had become their advisors.

The students quickly realized that they wanted cooperative leadership, so we flattened the traditional hierarchical model. Rick and I functioned more as their partners than their leaders, which worked just fine. Soon everyone was participating in group decisions, with pairs of people taking responsibility for each task—membership, hospitality, programming. They chose a convenor who took on the role of being a contact person for the group.

Our weekly meetings became wide-open discussions. What is sacred? Who/What is God? What is the meaning of life?

What does it mean to worship? Questions like these fit comfortably with the searching curiosity of college life. Speakers were invited to cover topics such as men's issues, employment as an expression of Unitarian Universalism, ecofeminism, Eastern religions and philosophies, the history of Unitarian Universalism, and more.

It was clear that the students needed a safe space on campus for exploring themselves, their values, and their spirituality. Here in the group they felt they could support one another and relax a little, even grow. At the time, this work didn't go by the name "ministry," but looking back, we see that's what it was.

From Andrea's point of view, a commitment to openness and inclusiveness captured the spirit of the group:

I remembered what it felt like to be disapproved of by some of the evangelical Christian students on campus. Our group focused personally on wanting to be inclusive and welcoming with everyone that we met. At the beginning of each semester, all religious organizations on campus would participate in a collective worship service that began with a processional of representatives from each campus religious group carrying that group's banner. In the case of some of the smaller groups, sometimes there wasn't a student available to carry their banner, so somebody from our group agreed to represent them in their absence. We were reaching out to others and actively living our belief that every group should be represented. Campus religious life was "whole-ly" only when all were there.

We were the only other student group who was willing to work with and fully support the Lambda Coalition (the campus support group for gay and lesbian students). Several women in our group posted flyers about the Lambda Coalition in dorms and fraternity houses. If you think this doesn't sound very brave or much like social action, you're wrong. The women who put up the flyers were subjected to name-calling and were spat upon by some men in some fraternities. We knew it was important to advertise everywhere: the gay members of those fraternity houses needed to know there were people who would support them coming out, if and when they chose to do so. Putting up the flyers was the right thing to do. Our campus needed a stronger Lambda Coalition.

As the weather turned cool, we planned a winter solstice celebration led by a member of the Unitarian Universalist Community Church in nearby Glen Allen. This was a new experience for many students—honoring a pagan, earth-based tradition. During the ceremony participants were led through a guided meditation and encouraged to find gifts inside that could be shared with the group. The event offered unexpected richness—the opening up of the spiritual and intellectual self to the beauty in all traditions, to the beauty of humanity.

In the fall of 1991 eleven of us went to the mountains for a weekend retreat. Margaret remembers:

The plan was to spend the first part of the weekend sharing stories of our personal spiritual journeys, the earliest memories of a spiritual self. Rick and I expected this to take about half a day. Instead, we spent most of the weekend in what turned out to be a deep and ambitious sharing activity. Laughter and tears came easily as members learned much about themselves and each other.

The weekend ended with everyone gathered on the deck overlooking the mountains. We shared readings and music to honor the sacredness of the time together and to invite hopes for the future. For some students, this was their first lay-led worship service ever. Given the climate on campus, this spirit of encouragement and growth was powerful and affirming.

After the retreat, trust continued to grow. College can be a complicated time as students deal with certain personal issues: relationships, sexuality and sexual orientation, acquaintance rape and sexual assault, divorce, death, alcohol and drug use/abuse issues, to name only a few. The group struggled with each of these issues and tried to talk openly and honestly, giving one another support in a quiet and safe setting away from the fast pace of daily routines and social life. Some weeks the whole time was spent on one subject. One member struggled through a date-rape trial, another questioned the fairness of her sorority discouraging a sister from bringing her girlfriend to a dance.

Someone else had parents going through a messy divorce. For each member the gathering offered the chance to process, to vent, to feel—without pressure to come up with an answer or feel a certain way. New friendships were created and old relationships deepened.

There was also a deepening of the relationship between the group and Margaret and Rick. Margaret recalls:

> *We were in our second year when my husband faced a medical crisis that affected the whole group. After the shocking diagnosis of multiple sclerosis, Rick was out of work for almost three months. Rick's walk was unsteady and his speech was slurred. We were stressed! Springing into action, the students made posters decorated with crazy and loving wishes to get well. They began weekly ice-cream excursions. Rick loved Italian gelato, and I loved that Rick was able to get out and do something he enjoyed. We didn't think they were doing anything so special, but now we know differently.*

All advisors attended monthly chaplaincy luncheons. Margaret shares her experience:

> *Here we learned how other campus groups were doing. As advisors we had signed a covenant to promote and support a healthy religious life on campus. Suddenly we discovered that this promise was changing our attitude toward the fundamentalist Christians we'd complained so much about. They became less*

*aggressive and we increased our respect for them. In
an annual overnight retreat, students and advisors
discussed the similarities and differences of Christianity, Islam, Judaism, Hinduism, and Unitarian Universalism.*

The group focused on quite a few social justice projects
and activities. Each year we spent a night sheltering homeless people at First Unitarian Church. Students spent time
sitting, talking, and playing cards with men and women
who found themselves homeless for one reason or another.
This evening of sheltering was a way for the students to
reach out beyond the "shelter" of the university walls and
make a small contribution to the needs of people in the
community. Andrea remembers:

*During that night talking with the homeless guests, I
realized how important support and community are.
Only if we are willing to talk with one another and
reach out to one another will healing begin on any
level—individually, within families, and in the
broader community. There we were as students reading the newspaper and looking for jobs. There were
our guests, people who were homeless, reading the
newspaper and looking for jobs. The parallels were
remarkable, yet the outcomes so different.*

We continued our work in social justice by attending
several major national marches in Washington, DC. Many

of the students had never been to a major march. We got up at 5:00 a.m. and almost everyone (except the driver and navigator) slept on the way up from Richmond. After lots of coffee, we parked the van in the Pentagon parking lot and got in the middle of the action. There we were, with other Unitarian Universalists! What a way to practice the democratic process. We were witnessing in the Unitarian Universalist way.

Andrea remembers when we attended a "Take Back the Night" march in Richmond:

The experience had profound significance for every member of our group, as many of us had spent time supporting individual members in recovery from sexual assault or date rape. I knew that the statistics held true, for one in four of my college friends had been raped. To gather together in the fight against sexual violence was an empowering emotional experience.

The university's campus ministry program was named "Journey to Wholeness." We counted close to twenty different campus religious groups among us. The chaplain's office gave wonderful support to us all, as individuals and as a group. We called ourselves the "Unitarian Universalist Student Community." Not all students joined First Unitarian Church in Richmond, but some did, and others joined another church after graduation. Many who didn't were still touched by the ministry of this group. Looking back, we don't think we talked that directly about the

Unitarian Universalist Principles and Purposes, but we put the principles into action in the group, on campus, and in the wider world. That was our ministry. And that is the best that religious community offers. One measure is that the University of Richmond's Unitarian Universalist Student Community continues today.

～

Margaret L. Beard is a lifelong Unitarian Universalist. A clinical social worker by training, she is now working for the UUA as Extension Ministry Director. Since her time at the University of Richmond, Andrea G. Dougherty completed a graduate degree in social work, moved to Wickford, RI, and is currently working as an outreach therapist for a mental health agency.

Ministry in the Maelstrom

Ed Cossum

When I retired, my wife Arlene and I decided to spend a significant part of our time participating in volunteer service. I was particularly interested in opportunities that would utilize my interest in carpentry and my enjoyment of physical labor. When Hurricane Hugo hit South Carolina in 1989, the call for volunteers seemed to match our interest and abilities.

Arlene and I were assigned to Summerville, South Carolina, a small rural community near Charleston. The mayor of Summerville had established a fledgling relief organization that eventually developed into the Dorchester Interfaith Outreach Ministries, which later won awards for distinguished service. The organization collected funds and building materials, filtered requests for aid, and coordinated volunteer assignments. It helped us locate a place to park our RV with electrical hookup. Our original plan to spend three weeks in Summerville at our own expense expanded to four trips of two to three weeks each when we realized the extent of the town's needs and the kind of support we could provide. When Arlene and I told our congregation what we were doing, two other members joined us for part of this time.

Our experiences in Summerville were especially rewarding. Not only did we help people repair their homes, we also contributed to their psychological recovery. Our first clients were a family who had retrieved the metal roof of their trailer after it had blown off, had put it back on, and were living under it, leaks and all. The walls and flooring were saturated with water. Their bedding, clothing, and furnishings were soaked, and the constant rain allowed no chance for anything to dry. When I first stepped into their trailer my foot went right through the floor. The family flatly refused our assessment that their trailer was unrepairable, and they would not accept the Red Cross's offer to pay for temporary housing. They had not asked for help but had been referred to us by a camp counselor for their son, who had throat cancer. It was clear that this family did not trust us or the Red Cross. They did agree to our covering their roof with tarpaper to provide temporary relief. We also replaced the damaged flooring in three rooms and got them fresh bedding from the Salvation Army. We later learned that the mother had been operating an egg business. She refused to tell this to the Federal Emergency Management Agency (FEMA), perhaps because she hadn't reported the income to the IRS, so we used $50 of our donated funds to buy 200 baby chicks for her.

As Arlene and I worked with this family, we learned that four of the mother's siblings lived in adjacent trailers that had also sustained damage. We were able to help two of them. Bea was in her mid-thirties with five children ranging from one-and-a-half to fifteen years old. She had lost part of her roof, several windows and doors, and the chimney of her heating stove. She had retrieved material from hurricane debris piled beside the road to make some repairs, but she needed additional help with her roof and stovepipe. She had lost all of the family's clothing, bedding, and most of their furniture from moisture and mildew. She had difficulty locating FEMA and the Red Cross because she couldn't read street signs, and when she did locate them she received no aid.

Arlene discovered that Bea's application to FEMA listed an incorrect amount for the private insurance she had collected. She had received $1,600 on a $7,000 policy, but FEMA had recorded her as receiving $16,000, making her ineligible for additional assistance. Arlene was able to get Bea clothing, bedding, and some furniture to replace what had been ruined. She also wrote and called Bea's insurance company and South Carolina's insurance commissioner, and Bea received another $4,000 to buy additional building materials to repair interior damage.

As Arlene gained Bea's confidence, we learned that Bea had been raised on a farm where her labor was more important to her family than her schooling. During Bea's childhood, local authorities did not enforce school attendance for black people. Bea had run away from home to live with an aunt in Charleston so she could attend school, but her parents had taken her back. Feeling the disempowerment of her illiteracy, Bea was eager to learn to read. With her consent, Arlene enrolled her in a literacy program and on our last trip to Summerville, Bea proudly showed us that she could read and write her name and a number of simple words.

Through our work in Summerville, we became familiar with many businesses in the community and were impressed by their altruism. The mayor owned one of the town's lumberyards, which was a "Nieman-Marcus" of lumberyards. His building materials and tools were of the highest quality, and his retail prices were significantly higher than his competition. However, he sold materials to the Dorchester Interfaith Outreach Ministries at cost, so that we could purchase high-quality materials when we couldn't get the material we needed from donated supplies. A local manufactured home dealer donated a damaged singlewide trailer and let us have odds and ends from his building supplies. When he didn't have all of the material we needed, he insisted that his supplier sell us windows and doors at prices lower than their price to him.

The local campground manager allowed volunteers to use their showers and allowed us to dump our septic tank at no charge. The three or four nights we stayed there were either free or deeply discounted. When I damaged a drainpipe by backing into rubbish, the local RV service spent hours replacing it and charged me for a fraction of their time. One cannot put a price on the boost that these heartwarming experiences gave us.

Although we appreciated our contacts with members of other faiths, Arlene and I missed the opportunity to share our experiences with other Unitarian Universalists. Only two members from our congregation had accompanied us, and the four of us were considered exceptions rather than representatives of our religion. At one point we were introduced to the Dorchester Interfaith Board as "good folks from a funky religion." This was not intended unkindly, but it did reflect their true impression.

The presence of more Unitarian Universalist volunteers and formal national sponsorship would have given a truer and more positive impression of the fundamental principles of our religion. We discovered that most mainline churches in South Carolina recognize the importance of helping members enrich themselves through volunteer service and have created organized disaster services. We were impressed by the Christian Reformed disaster service and decided that they would be a good model for us because their denomination is about the same size. In 1989 they had 800 volunteers signed up with identified skills and potential availability. They have formal training programs to certify volunteers for needs assessment, organize interfaith councils, offer psychological counseling, and coordinate repairs and reconstruction.

After our experiences with Hurricane Hugo, Arlene and I decided to start a Unitarian Universalist disaster service. In 1990 we did so under the sponsorship of the UUA Florida District. I believed that our primary clients would be other Unitarian Universalists who would want to volunteer for disaster recovery and would value the opportunity to do so as Unitarian Universalists. Two years later my belief was validated when more than 200 Unitarian Universalists volunteered to assist in recovery work after Hurricane Andrew hit the Florida coast. Almost without exception, these volunteers experienced a sense of accomplishment by helping others in need, especially since most of our effort was directed toward people who had been in need even before the hurricane. The physical repairs we made were essential, but our presence was at least as valuable. On more than one occasion someone whose home had been devastated, but who had saved what they could in a dry corner, told us, "We are grateful for your coming, but we're okay. Please help someone who needs it more." The converse was also true. On one occasion we were late discovering a Unitarian Universalist in need, and the person suffered devastating feelings of aloneness.

Disaster recovery enables one to witness humanity at its worst and best. The worst were instances in which individuals vandalized property or took money for false promises of repair work and then disappeared. Two churches attempted to use our disaster recovery service for their own benefit instead of for those most in need. Fortunately, these examples were far overshadowed by the many instances of great generosity. One Unitarian Universalist couple provided housing for the first month that Arlene and I worked after Hurricane Andrew, and they answered dozens of phone calls from prospective volunteers and victims. They even offered their hospitality for the duration of our stay, knowing that it would be for many months. We were able to establish headquarters in our RV closer to the greatest need, but their generosity was sincerely appreciated.

Many people of all faiths offered housing for volunteers or victims when their own homes had been less affected. Military members on duty in the area volunteered their free time to help victims. One day I saw two enlisted men with rifles slung across their shoulders carrying bags of ice as they walked along cheerfully with an elderly woman. They had been distributing ice from a truck and, realizing that she could not carry it herself, volunteered to carry it for her.

Being unfamiliar with the Florida community, Arlene and I needed to work through a local organization for client selection, volunteer housing, and numerous other services. An interfaith council was just being organized and would take months to become effective. We formed a partnership with Centro Campesino, which had been working with migrant farm workers for over twenty years, and our alliance became more mutually beneficial as time went on. Unitarian Universalist volunteers were housed at Centro, initially in tents, and eventually in a house built with Unitarian Universalist funds and volunteers from all faiths. Volunteers from other faiths working through Centro provided continuity on major projects that we would not have been able to undertake with our limited volunteer and financial resources.

We also participated in weekly Red Cross briefings of

volunteer services. We shared experiences with others, were updated on FEMA and local building department policies, gained access to Salvation Army and Church World Service supplies, and occasionally took Red Cross assignments. Our participation brought visibility to our faith, something that had not happened in South Carolina. One Red Cross volunteer, also a Unitarian Universalist, noticed the shirts we had made for our volunteers to identify us as Unitarian Universalists. He had worked for years to get the UUA interested in direct volunteer service, but never expected it to happen.

Although Centro Campesino focused on assisting migrant farm workers and providing low-cost housing for those who were permanent residents, they had never worked with the predominantly black local community. As a result of Hurricane Andrew, they became interested in expanding their services to that community and asked for our help since we also were interested in helping there. They sent Arlene to local churches to offer new shoes that Centro had in excess. The Covenant Missionary Baptist Church was distributing food and clothing and accepted Centro's offer. Arlene then used our contact with the Red Cross to obtain cleaning supplies and other items for the church's free store.

One memorable client was a seventy-seven-year-old widow who had lived through the storm alone in her home while windows, doors, carport, and pieces of roof blew away. When asked what she did during the storm, she replied that she had had a long conversation with Him. She is accustomed to conversing with Him and believes that He intervened to save her life when the bedroom door blew off and careened down the hall where she had just been standing. With the help of a deacon from her church and many other volunteers, we gradually renovated her house to the point where she says it looks better than when it was new.

Our favorite client was a seventy-six-year-old widow living in her condemned home with a leaky roof, boarded-up windows, and no power or gas. She was reluctant to accept our help, but a deacon in her church helped us persuade her to rebuild. We bought a shed for most of her belongings and were able to arrange for a trailer from FEMA to be parked next to her house for her to live in during the reconstruction. We thought that she would be so distressed to see her old home destroyed that we arranged for the wife of her deacon to take her home with them. She would have none of that! She worked right along with us, carrying broken boards and other debris to the street and amazing all of the volunteers.

We discovered that she was a one-person "Salvation Army." Her home was filled with clothing that she had collected for distribution to others in the community. She also collected aluminum cans and donated the proceeds to the church. She had difficulty realizing that her new home was a gift and kept asking when she would get her coupon book to begin payments. She attempted to volunteer at Centro, but when they were unable to use her, she volunteered at a food bank. As we came to know her, we realized that her character was recognized throughout the community as well as in her church.

I wish every Unitarian Universalist, in fact people of every faith, could have had the privilege we had of living and working with people of such diverse religious, cultural, and economic backgrounds. Most of the people we helped showed an amazing generosity of spirit and ability to cope or rise above their circumstances. Not every volunteer shared in the same experiences, but everyone did have the satisfaction of knowing that they had made a difference in someone's life, and many became acquainted with and gained respect for the people they helped. Many also had the opportunity to work with volunteers of other religious beliefs who shared a common concern for the victims of the disaster. We also witnessed the continuing disaster that many human beings experience in their everyday lives. A fence blown away by Hurricane Andrew revealed a shantytown that had been hidden from the community. We wondered what it would take to break down the fences in our hearts that allow such conditions to exist here and all over the world.

Many enriching service opportunities exist if we look for them. Disaster service can utilize almost anyone, and for as little or as much as one is able to commit to. It requires no special skill. Anyone who can drive can provide transportation for victims or run errands for construction volunteers. Others who have dealt with an insurance company or a government agency have the ability to help victims cope with the FEMA and Red Cross bureaucracies.

Disaster service isn't for the faint of heart, though! It requires enormous patience and stubborn insistence to cope with FEMA, building departments, and other bureaucracies, and clean-up, demolition, and construction can be dangerous.

When Arlene and I first proposed a disaster service to the Unitarian Universalist Association, we were asked, "Why is it important for the UUA or individual congregations to provide opportunities for service? Isn't worship the sole function of a religious institution?" The most suitable answer I can think of comes from a minister in Greensboro, Alabama. During an evening prayer meeting for his congregation and volunteers who were rebuilding a black church that had burned under suspicious circumstances, he criticized the "edifice complex" that causes congregations to focus on the church building rather than on service to their community. He chastised members of all churches for being satisfied with rejuvenating themselves on Sunday mornings through worship and then ignoring opportunities for service the rest of the week. He likened this to getting our car filled with gas without intending to drive it anywhere. Would it make sense for a church to provide the inspiration for service and then rely on other institutions to provide the opportunity? What kind of witness to our beliefs would that be?

Jimmy Carter once said, "Rosalynn and I thought that we were making a sacrifice when we agreed to work for Habitat for Humanity. Rather than a sacrifice, this has been the most rewarding experience of our lives." Arlene and I feel the same about our disaster services, and comments from other volunteers are similar. We have learned and gained from this experience far out of proportion to our effort.

The interdependent web of all existence provides both the necessity and the reward of being our siblings' keepers, and direct service is an opportunity to feel the reward immediately and at first hand.

~

Ed Cossum is the founder and coordinator of the Florida District UUA Disaster Service since 1989.

Ministry in Words

Julio Noboa Polanco

From my upbringing, I knew that living a religion meant much more than going to church once a week or swearing by a certain creed. Keeping the faith meant living it every day in ordinary as well as extraordinary circumstances.

As I reflect on my work history, it is astounding to see how much my work actually influences the lives of other people. Much of my professional life involves a form of "ministry." If done well, my work can help fulfill the material or emotional needs of many with whom I have little or no direct contact.

Born in a public city hospital in a Bronx barrio, I never stayed in the Big Apple long enough to call it home. My parents came, as did so many other immigrants, looking for freedom, opportunity, and a better life. They worked hard, went to church, and thrived in their ethnic and religious community. Yet, my parents never forgot their homeland, the island of Puerto Rico. Throughout their lives, they spoke about the tropical paradise they had lost as though it were a warm innocence replaced by the cold reality of New York City.

They spoke poetically about the beauty of the land, its lush vegetation, and the incomparable flavor of its fresh native produce. They described with dignified pride a strong, secure sense of family and community in their small town. With a bittersweet nostalgia for their paradise lost, my parents' generation bemoaned the passing of their golden age as they saw their precious island become mechanized, modernized, and Americanized.

My parents eventually moved back to the island, but not before spending over three decades in another big city, Chicago. There, I went to public schools for most of my early years. I enrolled at the University of Illinois Circle Campus and majored in anthropology. At first I had romantic notions of going to faraway lands and completing an ethnography, à la Margaret Mead, of some exotic tribe to uncover its quaint customs and profound secrets. Later, I saw more practical value just in having been trained in ethnographic methods. After five years of full-time work, my formal education continued at Northwestern University, where I enrolled in an educational anthropology program and eventually earned a master's degree in education.

Pivotal as this formal education was for every aspect of my intellectual and occupational life, it was really in my work that I truly engaged with the world and became transformed by it. Like most youngsters who enter the work force, my initial motive was earning money. It was only in the process of becoming involved with my tasks and coworkers that some sense of personal satisfaction set in. There grew in me a sense of interest for what I did. Eventually I realized that one of the greatest benefits of working was in gaining knowledge, skills, and even some measure of wisdom. Gradually I looked beyond my own personal development and growth, and it became clear that whatever I earned was in some direct or indirect way of benefit to my family, especially since both my parents had had to work outside the home to support me and my two sisters.

About the time that I started developing a sense of ethnic identity and pride, I realized the implications of being one of the few Latino professionals employed in a department or institution. It meant that I was expected to speak for my people, to explain our culture, manners, traditions, and problems to people who looked to me for answers. I reluctantly became the representative of a Puerto Rican to many who had never worked with Latinos. Because whatever I did or said reflected on my community, I decided that I would do what I could in my job to advocate for the rights and dignity of *el pueblo*, my people.

Beyond the money or personal growth and satisfaction, I came to understand work as something that contributed to a cause greater than myself. I was most satisfied when my work contributed to a struggle to achieve certain ideals, such as equity, justice, and truth. Needless to say, this didn't involve me in the most lucrative occupations. I found that the more dedicated or altruistic the work I performed, the lower the salary and benefits I received.

In May 1995, I had the opportunity to write a biweekly column for the *San Antonio Express-News*, a major daily newspaper that covers San Antonio and all of South Texas. My initial motive for writing the column was to release my anger and frustration at being bombarded with bigoted, ignorant, and conservative views in every medium. I wanted to challenge these perspectives with a progressive Latino voice rarely heard in the mass media. But as I struggled to find my written voice and to articulate my world-view, my initial anger was contained and diminished. I found that expressing myself from an emotional or vindictive source of energy only added to the fuel of intolerance and fanned the flames of discord.

To react with anger in the face of injustice, hypocrisy, and fallacy violated all the valuable lessons I had learned through my experiences. My anger had not totally dissipated, but it had stopped being the energizing force of my expression. Gradually a much greater sense of mission set in. It was no longer important to refute, contradict, or challenge; it was more significant to inform, educate, persuade, and even inspire.

As I started receiving responses to my column, both positive and negative, something dawned on me. I realized the indisputable power of the written word. Growing within me was a deep, almost overwhelming, sense of responsibility. The mere thought that thousands, if not tens of thousands, throughout San Antonio and South Texas were reading my columns made me reconsider even more carefully what and how I would write. Being a responsible columnist entailed more than resourceful research and skillful writing. Beyond style I had to have substance; beyond facts I had to have wisdom.

One of the greatest joys as a columnist is receiving calls from women and men who simply thank me for having expressed what I did. Whether or not they agree with me, calls from well-informed people are always an educational experience. Especially satisfying are the calls I get from Latinos, including some barrio folk, who almost liken me to a folk hero for taking on the mighty powers that be.

So where's the ministry in this? Writing a column is a kind of ministry because it's similar to a sermon. But instead of seeking a foundation in and inspiration from a holy book, dogma, creed, or denomination, I strive to reflect the qualities found in all genuine faiths and philosophies: justice, truth, equality, and humanity. My work is a ministry of words, ideas, and perspectives.

I am also engaged in another ministry of words: the field of education. Public education is a vital element of our society, and teachers are the focal point of the educational process. As a clinical supervisor and instructor with the University of Northern Iowa, I supervise student teachers in their final semester before they obtain a teaching certificate. To supervise student teachers at this final stage of their development is to contribute to a life-transforming experience that will help establish a teacher's attitude and style for decades to come.

With my colleague and senior partner, Dr. Christine Canning, we design, create, and facilitate an urban, multicultural experience for these Iowa college students who have had little or no contact with children of color. We host guest speakers, provide structured experiences and multicultural events, and facilitate in-depth discussions on racial, gender, disability, socioeconomic, and cross-cultural issues. Our student teachers are required to reflect, in both writing and discussion, on their own biases, prejudices, and assumptions. This process of self-examination is never easy; it involves a level of introspection that is often painful and disturbing for our students.

Yet in this process we assist them as mentors, guides, and supporters so that we can model some of the qualities that caring educators bring to their work. Ultimately, this ministry of personal and professional transformation never ceases to affect us as well as the students themselves.

In the decades to come, a growing number of children of color will be taught by Anglo teachers. We hope to develop models of training that can help prepare European American teachers to be more sensitive, understanding, and effective in dealing with children of color. Because a significant proportion of our nation's future work force will be African American, Latino, Asian, and other workers of color, the education of all children regardless of class, race, gender, or ethnicity is of vital interest to our entire society. A healthy, viable, friendly, mutually beneficial, and respectful relationship between an Anglo teacher and a student of color would help ensure a peaceful and prosperous future for our society.

It has been my distinct opportunity and challenge to

help this relationship flourish among the people I work with. This is a ministry and a mission whose ultimate effects and benefits will endure long after I am a remote memory in the minds of future teachers.

Both of my ministries are closely interrelated. Through writing and education I can help my society deal with the difficult issues of diversity, inclusion, and equity. These challenges will reverberate well into the next millennium. If there is to be a new age of harmony and understanding, it will happen, not through magical means, but through the good work each of us does with dignity, conviction, and heart.

~

Julio Noboa Polanco is a writer and educator living in San Antonio, Texas. He is a columnist for the San Antonio Express-News *and is a Clinical Supervisor with the Department of Teaching at the University of Northern Iowa. His speeches, writing, and research focus on topics in education, cultural diversity, and social justice.*

Social Justice as Lay Ministry

Mary-Ella Holst

In October I will be deep in glue, glitter, and feathers as Halloween approaches at the Booker T. Washington Learning Center. Its after-school program serves twenty-four children with homework help, activities, special projects, and a hot meal. Most of the children are in some form of foster care. By late November, I will shop and bake for our Christmas/Kwanzaa celebration. During Black History Month I will scan magazines for photos of historic African American figures as school reports come due. My own grandchildren will call me to similar bursts of attention and activity. It is predictable and unpredictable, the same colors of construction paper punctuated by a sudden smile.

My church is the Unitarian Church of All Souls, in New York City. We have an established and active social outreach program, including an AIDS task force that has received national recognition. We have feeding programs to serve people in our own neighborhood, a scouting program in East Harlem that leads eight troops from Brownies to Cadets, and Cubs to training for Eagle Scouts, plus other programs including our work with the Booker T. Washington Learning Center where I volunteer.

This churchwide effort needs many volunteers and a lot of money. We obtain funding through the work of women and men who have created an auction so successful and appealing to the public that it has generated its own philanthropic organization—the Heart and Soul Foundation, Inc. Volunteer Michelle Jawin is a lawyer and mother who leads (she would say "nudges") a dedicated group that each year raises money to support those of us working face-to-face with people. I consider Michelle Jawin a partner in my social justice ministry.

What is the difference between a volunteer and a lay minister? Many of us share a commitment to the goal of social justice, but not all volunteers are on the road to what we call "ministry." Volunteers make a measurable contribution to the life of the community, and the work can be interesting, even fun. Ministry has traditionally been termed a "call," a prompting of the spirit that cannot be resisted. This idea developed into our concept of "vocation"—a word we don't hear much anymore in discussions of jobs and careers. Social justice is not my job; it never has been. My career has often been aligned with it but I would not call it my profession. My search for social justice is a prompting of the spirit to which I have responded with increasing awareness of the forces that shape individual lives and communities.

As I walk down 101st Street toward the Center I will

see the church where we meet in the basement and across the street a ball field and a narrow strip of land that is our annex set amidst a community garden. But I will also see the block as it was eight years ago, just another abandoned lot filled with scrapped automobiles and junkies doing business on shredded car seats. I will know what it took to transform the block—the community effort, the leadership, the negotiation, the maze of bureaucracy, $250,000 for the annex alone. If today I am headed for computers in the annex, I will walk through roses, trees, and a patch of ripening pumpkins where there once was broken glass, toxic soil, and used needles.

I will attend several Unitarian Universalist Service Committee (UUSC) board meetings in their Cambridge, Massachusetts, headquarters. While I am in the reception area, I will enjoy yet another detail in the ceramic Children's Wall created by artist Judith Inglese. Before the board convenes, I will attend the investment committee meeting where a small percentage difference in returns can affect human rights and social justice programs around the world. With the other members of the board I will review accomplishments and plans for national and international programs while trying to budget effectively.

In November 1996, I represented the UUSC at ceremonies in Tokyo and Osaka, Japan, to mark the fiftieth anniversary of Licensed Agencies for Relief in Asia (LARA). Back in 1946 we were one of thirteen nongovernmental agencies, including the AFL-CIO, American Friends Service Committee, Catholic Relief Services, the YMCA and the YWCA, as well as Japanese-American organizations, that shipped 200 boatloads of clothing, foodstuffs, and medical supplies to the Japanese people. This material was distributed to 10 million people through orphanages, homes for the elderly, and other institutions. At the anniversary celebration we heard Japanese speakers tell stories about what this relief actually meant in their lives. For instance, I learned that when it had arrived, the powdered milk was a puzzle: it had never been seen before in Japan.

In Tokyo we visited a home for children that was founded in 1945 when a Tokyo mother took in a three-year-old boy she found abandoned in war rubble. Today thirty children live here, four to six to a bedroom. The supervisor, who is the daughter of the original founder, sleeps in the bedroom of the smallest children so that "they will never be alone." After our visit, as we stood outside on the quiet suburban street, I thought I heard wind-chimes. Within a few moments children returning from school came into view. There were about seven of them, and the sound I had heard was their happy voices—the excitment of release from school and coming home.

In Osaka we toured a recently remodeled community center that offered daycare, after-school care, night care for women who work at late hours, and activities for the elderly (including an impressive hot bath!). Here, the play-house was shaped like a tea house. This beautiful spacious building represents the most advanced thinking in design and architecture for human services. As I wandered around, I was comparing the facility to the Booker T. Washington Learning Center, since the services are similar. I remembered that the Japanese constitution limits defense spending to 5 percent of the annual budget. The tour reinforced the importance of policies and priorities committed to social welfare.

Advocacy, hard to dramatize, is the hidden component of social change in a democratic society. There are few visuals to convey the importance of writing letters, or meeting with anonymous staff aides of your local congressperson, or wading through lengthy position papers. This is advocacy. And if you do it right, which means doing it carefully and consistently, it is effective.

My work takes me all over. Wherever I am, I try to be certain that the children of East Harlem and their families inform my discussions in Cambridge, and that UUSC's concept of partnership guides my actions in East Harlem. I hope to make choices in my own life with integrity based upon its entirety: my family—past, present, and future; my education—formal and informal; and my experience. I do what I believe needs to be done to bring social justice and human rights to the children, women, and men in this complex partnership we have named life. I do it because I can't resist the call of the spirit toward justice. I will not lay it down.

~

Mary-Ella Holst, Director of Religious Education Emerita of the Unitarian Church of All Souls, New York City, is a poet as well as an activist. A collection of her work was published as Beyond Dreams of Rescue *(Wind Rose Press, 1992), and she is included in* Unitarian Universalist Poets: A Contemporary American Survey *(Pudding House Press, 1996).*

~ Serving in New Ways

Paul Just Died

Laila D. Ibrahim

I was sitting at my desk in my cubicle when Shirley told me the news: "Paul just died." I wandered over to the main office area to sit with everyone else in silence. No one knew what to do. After a few moments, though, we started to discuss how best to support our coworker Les whose partner had just died of AIDS. It was clear to us that Les would like some visitors, so three of us decided to go to his home where Paul had been able to die. I started to make a list of people in the office from whom we could collect money for groceries and flowers to bring with us.

"How do you know how to do this?" Shirley asked me. *Do what?* I thought to myself. Then I thought about the meals I coordinated among my office workers to bring to Les, I thought about the time I spent listening to Les talk about Paul's all-too-quick deterioration, and I thought about the theological questions I raised about death with my coworkers. "Church," I said. "I learned how to care for people during difficult times in church."

It became clear to me at that moment that my lay pastoral ministry extended into every aspect of my life and was now an important part of my work. I had been involved in the pastoral associates program at my church, one of six laypeople who had been trained to do pastoral care for members of the congregation in need. Our training focused primarily on developing listening skills, learning ways of providing instrumental support, such as childcare and meals, and most important, gaining a sense of authority as pastoral ministers. One of my fellow pastoral associates could not emphasize enough that although our pastoral work in the church was important, our pastoral work outside the church, especially in our work settings, was even more important. Since I was a college student at the time and had had no full-time work experience, I didn't understand what he meant.

What I didn't know in college that I learned as a full-time worker was that for many people, work is their primary, perhaps even their only, community. My coworkers didn't have full extended families nearby nor did they attend church or synagogue. Their community consisted of the people who happened to do the same work that they did. On a daily basis they received support from their coworkers or not at all.

And I was working with a group of people who needed a lot of support. In the three years I worked in that office we had, among other things, three people caring for someone with AIDS, a man who underwent prostate surgery, a person waiting for an international adoption to come through, and a woman dealing with the breakup of her long-term partnership. There were only twelve people in my work group. Those twelve people were facing critical life issues. I spent a lot of time simply listening to my co-workers talk about the struggles in their lives. Fortunately, I had a fair amount of flexibility in my position so that I could do this. I know that my listening contributed to the morale of the workplace and most likely to productivity, too. In addition, it was a way I could put my values and beliefs into action and teach other people about those values.

I value being a caring witness to another's pain. I know that the world often is cruel and hard. It also can be loving and supportive. We have little control over the cruel and hard aspects of life such as disease, infertility, and loss. But we humans have the capacity to make the world more loving and supportive by offering community. While some may look to a loving God to ease life's pains, I believe that we are the primary instruments of a loving God and are responsible for the creation of a more compassionate world. The work of creating a compassionate world does not belong to a select few. It is the responsibility and privilege of us all.

Human beings have an innate ability to be empathetic. We are social beings who care about maintaining the well-being of others. Professionally I am now an early childhood educator. In my work I see how children who have been emotionally supported respond to the emotional distress of other children. They will come get a teacher to help a child who has fallen, they will kiss an "owie" on their friend, or they will sing a song to support a child who is sad about saying good-bye to a parent.

As we age we seem to lose faith in our ability to be appropriately responsive to the pain of others. I think this happens for a number of reasons. The first is that when our pain is dismissed it is more difficult to empathize with others and we become more hardened to the world around us. Another dynamic is that as we age we become aware of all of the pain in the world and become overwhelmed by it. There is so much pain, so much injustice, and so much to do to make this world into our ideal of a welcoming, supportive community that we feel paralyzed about where to begin. And finally I think we are afraid of making mistakes. We are afraid we will say the wrong thing. We are afraid we will pry where we are not wanted. We are afraid that we will offend.

We can learn to overcome each of these difficulties. If you have a hard time being open and empathetic to others because no one has listened to your pain and given you emotional support, you gradually can learn to be more comfortable with pain, both your own and that of others. Often people feel overwhelmed by and afraid of other people's emotions because we have been taught that once emotions are unleashed they are uncontrollable. Too readily we want to support people by being constructive and working out a solution to the problem. While people need such support eventually, what they initially need most is simply to express their feelings to a caring listener. Some pain can't be "solved"; it just needs to be lived through. By being open to your own pain and that of others you learn that for most people pain does end, or at least diminishes, and that expressing your pain helps you to get through the difficult time. By practicing being a witness to another's pain and also expressing your pain to others, you help a community break the cycle of dismissing people's pain.

If you feel overwhelmed by the vastness of pain, I say pick your pain. No one person can attend to all the pain in the world. But if each of us focuses on something we feel passionate about, then we can create a better place for all of us. Some people focus their energy on attending to the needs of people in Bosnia, others focus their ministry on the plight of the homeless in this country, and others minister to families who are living with personal loss. Each is a necessary ministry, and each contributes to easing the pain in this world. You can't do it all by yourself, but what you do contributes something invaluable to the whole.

If you are concerned about making mistakes, I say it is better to appear awkward and foolish than callous and uncaring. A person in pain would rather receive bumbling attempts at care than feel isolated and invisible. Like anything worth doing ministry takes practice. It is a skill that you can cultivate and grow. It won't necessarily feel safe or comfortable at first, but with some training and practice you will know how to carefully listen to, watch for, and attend to the struggles of the people around you.

And, by example, you can teach others to do the same. Pay attention to the people around you. Ask them about who and what matters to them. What are the sorrows in their lives? If you listen carefully they will tell you. Remember to ask again weeks, months, and sometimes years after a loss. Anniversaries of losses are difficult times that regularly go unnoticed.

Think about appropriate ways to mark passages in people's lives: births, graduations, deaths, recovery, and so on. In the work setting organize birthday events that are appropriate for your setting. A baby shower at work may be the only way a new parent receives much of the necessary and expensive equipment for his baby. Invite a coworker to have lunch with you so you can hear about the major transition in her life.

Organizing meals for a coworker in need is a great way to create a sense of community and care in your work setting. Many people will be grateful for the opportunity to do something helpful. Some people will need assurance that their meal does not have to be perfect and that anything will be a welcome gesture.

As the people you work with see you building community and taking care of others, they will begin to do the same. They will see work as a place where support is given and received. Sometimes they will be in a position to give care and other times they will be the one receiving care. If you are in a community long enough you see that the cycle of giving and receiving, supporting and being supported is ongoing. It doesn't begin or end with any one person.

A few months ago I heard the news that Les had died. He was attended by a home hospice nurse and two of his former coworkers. If his coworkers hadn't been there he would have died attended only by a stranger who had never known his whole self. It wasn't an easy death, but it was a good death, helped by the ministry his coworkers gave him. Ministry to others is a God-given gift that we can all have if we accept it. May more of us choose to do so.

~

Laila D. Ibrahim is a member of the First Unitarian Church of Oakland, California, and has been an active Unitarian Universalist since she was thirteen. She lives in Berkeley with her partner and two daughters. By profession she is an early childhood educator.

Youth as Ministers to Each Other

Kathryn Deal

I usually get a few blank stares when I ask kids to describe how they minister to each other. "You mean like our minister at church?" Most young people think ministry is what they see on Sunday mornings. While they may not use the word, however, ministry is at the heart of their connection in our faith community.

Unitarian Universalist high schoolers, kids between the ages of fourteen and eighteen or so, are represented and served at the district level by Young Religious Unitarian Universalists (YRUU). Here is the covenant created by one district's YRUU: "As we come to this YRUU event we are committed: to be ourselves, to be there for others, to be respectful of the environment, to maintain an open community, to be inclusive." These are the goals of successful youth ministry. Through the creation of a safe environment, youth find their social and spiritual identity. In a community that members are expected to enter with open heart and open mind, youth have the chance to experience ministering to themselves and to others.

Some kids in youth groups worry about being ostracized because they are different—maybe they are "brains," or kids who look different than the popular standard; perhaps their parents don't make much money, or they make too much. Youth fear being different. The challenge for everyone in our congregations is to live out the belief in each person's worth and dignity. Our youth groups try to foster the expectation that everyone is accepted. Youth groups work hard to guard against the cliques that are usually so strong in the school environment. In this ministry of acceptance youth's spirituality grows.

I hear teens speak of their church youth camps as sacred spaces—places where they are free to laugh and cry, hug and scream, sing and dance without fear of the judgments that they sometimes face in school and family settings. A teen once asked me, "If the adults really believe in the inherent worth and dignity of every person, why do they judge us by our outer selves?" Youth are checking out the consequences of their actions and appearances. They are also daring adults to challenge them, so that they have a chance to rebel. In doing this, they create an age-appropriate distance from old ideas. They are seeking ideas of their own.

Through worship, social action, learning, and leadership, teens can experience the building blocks of community: bonding, affirming, opening up, stretching, sharing, and setting goals. Such steps in community building are taught to both the teens and adults at Unitarian Universalist youth leadership development conferences. It is important to know these steps so that when there is a problem, with cliques for instance, you can bring the group back to the basics. It is always good at the beginning of the school year for groups to return to the first steps of bonding and affirming before going on with the business of the year.

Bonding is the first stage, when people don't really know each other. For example, adults are bonding when they say, "Hi, how are you?" at the beginning of a committee meeting or when setting up for a spaghetti dinner. In bonding we recognize and acknowledge one another and the environment.

Affirming happens when the youth are all sharing and having fun together and seeing that they have things in common. Take Sharon and Tony as an example. When Sharon found out that her parents were planning to divorce, she felt set apart, a bit different from the others. Tony's parents were also getting divorced. These two kids, with not much else in common, got to talking while they were preparing for the youth talent show.

"I can't wait for them to stop fighting."

"Me too! I'm going through the same thing at my house!"

This me-too communication is paramount in building youth community. Youth need affirmation that they are okay and that others are going through some of the same experiences.

The need for me-too affirming shows up in many youth group activities. Some Native Americans use the word *ho* in talking circles to signify agreement. Many teens I've worked with have adopted this gesture of agreement—discussion groups and in worship services. I hear other affirmative expressions—"Hear, hear," "Cool!," "I'm with you"—used in the same way. Some kids have adopted the American Sign Language sign for "yes." Others rub their hands together to show approval or acceptance of some part of a worship service or other quiet moment.

Though members of all age groups have ways of affirming each other, youth have adapted and codified ways to communicate approval. Among teens there seems to be an intrinsic need for these behaviors.

John was a kid who never received a lot of strokes when growing up. Being gay was something his family could not yet accept. But the youth group affirmed John by continuing to include him and be loving to him. When John first showed up at youth group, he was cool and isolated, staying separated from the others. Some wondered why he bothered to come at all. Someone else explained, "He needs acceptance." Indeed he did. John began to drop the act, to open up. Affirmation changed John's life.

During check-ins, individuals are invited to *open up* and share their feelings. This goes hand-in-hand with affirmations. Laura, who joined the group a bit later than some of the others, wasn't sure how much she had in common with them or if she even wanted to be part of the group. Laura was sitting quietly when Jennifer spoke up during the initial check-in: "I don't really feel like I know anyone here. I am shy when it comes to new groups and I seem to push people away. I guess that's just how I am. But I do want to make friends."

Hearing this, Laura relaxed a bit. She said, "I agree with . . . Jennifer. . . . Is that your name? Yeah, well, I feel the same way. I feel like super new to all this. You guys seem to really know each other. Now I know I am not the only one. Thanks, Jennifer, for helping me express what I was feeling."

Opening up can be either as light as "I had a bad day" or as heavy as "I am lonely when I am not at church." It can take many forms and is the basis for trust in youth ministry.

Stretching happens in the group when they find that they may not agree on everything, but they can still get along. Accepting individual differences for the larger need of the group is an important step in the group's maturity level. In our youth group, there were two best friends I'll call Lilly and Rose. They claimed to have everything in common. "We are exactly alike!" they would say. "I couldn't live without her!" Rose would say of Lilly. Then Lilly got a boyfriend and spent every minute with him. Rose started writing poetry and short stories. They both found new places in relation to the world. But could they still be friends? Not without stretching.

Stretching is forgiveness, plain and simple. It is also a growing acceptance of self in relationship to others. Stretching means, "What I do is OK, even if others do it differently." It is more a gradual piecing together of values that make the youth individual and distinct from each other.

Shawn and Justine were great friends until Shawn started smoking. Would they be great friends afterward? Only if there was stretching on both sides, an effort made to understand the other's opinions, to understand why they behave as they do and to make considerations for the other. Stretching in a group is like the physical practice of yoga. To be mastered, stretching must happen over and over, slowly and with love.

Deeper *sharing* and *goal-setting* happen as the group grows to trust and depend on one another. Sometimes a crisis can initiate the change, such as a car accident, or a few in the group being arrested, or a death in the family or some other trouble. One member's crisis can cause the whole group to move to a more advanced stage of ministering to one another.

Although youth have a tendency to be hard on each other, I have seen this deeper sharing more often among youth than among adults. I remember a sixteen-year-old boy who ran away from home after his older brother had beaten him bloody. Every kid in the youth group asked his or her parents if the boy could stay with them for a week until the situation could be handled by the proper authorities. Finally, one youth stepped forward and offered him a place to stay long enough to finish out his senior year in school. These kids were immediate in their protective response. They rallied around him, and all of them found a bit more to live for. The group had evolved as they ministered.

In another group, a dying pet catalyzed ministry to one another. A girl and her best friend from the youth group held a pet dog as it died in their arms in the vet's office. The friend called the youth group at church (they were meeting when this happened). The group left the church immediately and met up with the two friends, bringing ice cream along. They played music while the girl cried. They massaged her back and listened to her. They were all changed by this experience.

Some teen trouble seems too overwhelming to acknowledge. I met Victor through district youth activities. We all looked up to him—he was on the football team, surfed, and was regarded as "one cool dude." We ignored his drug problem, thinking we couldn't help. When I went to Victor's funeral years later, I wondered if we could have done more. He was only thirty when he died. Could our group have taken a stand back then? We ministered to ourselves by sticking together, and that made the group closer. But we did not help our weakest link. Who could have helped? One of us? An adult? The worry stays with me.

It is important for the group to be able to step back to include new members. They may not notice that their depth of sharing and ministering can make a newcomer feel left out. They may see cliques forming but not understand what to do. At this point a helpful adult may be able to keep the group intact to minister to each other.

Youth minister each other through a variety of activities. One is worship. A youth worship service is unique. For example, the term *fellowship* instead of *worship* is frequently used to describe youths' services because the emotional connection that the youth make during their services is usually linked to their affirmations of each other's perspective and life experience. During youth fellowship services, usually everyone sits or stands in a circle. This allows all present to be have an opportunity to be with each other. Like Quaker worship, everyone can share when and if they wish. This structure balances individuality and group identity.

Worship also provides structure. Sometimes our Unitarian Universalist youth want more answers than we think. One young woman once said to me, "I need answers sometimes! There are so many questions that this church asks of the individual! For once, I would like the safety of an answer." Youth need and want boundaries. If they don't have them, they will try to test them and make their own. It is the same with ritual. Ritual is beneficial because it gives people something they can rely on to happen even when the rest of the world has gone haywire. Grace, readings, meditations, songs, and lighting the chalice are all ways to create a safe, known place that youth need for their sharing and accepting of each other.

One young man's father was a devout atheist. Growing up, the father had advised the son never to talk to people about God—because there was no such thing. This did not help the young man develop the skills he needed for talking about his beliefs. Instead, he rebelled against his father and was firmly entrenched in his own belief of God.

We Unitarian Universalists need to develop skills for talking about our beliefs. Youth easily spot close-mindedness and hypocrisy and the results can alienate the youngster from the faith community. Youth need role models to hold on to, and we adults must realize more fully the power of our deeds.

Social action gives young people another opportunity to minister to each other and to heal themselves, as well as the chance to connect with causes outside their every-day circle. Social action can provide a bond for teens who otherwise may have little in common. By making service the center of any church's youth curriculum, we build habits and ethics of service into the future of Unitarian Universalism.

Sometimes young people know that they want to be involved in social action but don't know where to start. Many of them have the energy and time, but they feel a bit helpless. Adults have the habit of telling youth it's their turn to help change the world, but this can be a daunting message to hear. The best projects are ones in which youth can feel a high level of success and through which they bond with each other and the larger world.

Our youth also minister to each other through the lead-ership roles in their youth groups on the local and district level. At a recent board meeting of my district's YRUU group, I watched the elections for various board positions. Each youth who was nominated stood up to say why she or he wanted this particular leadership role.

"I have gotten a lot out of YRUU over the past couple

of years," one nominee said. "It's now time for me to give back to the group. I like being at the pulse of what is happening in the district. I like being a role model for other people that are younger than me in the same way that someone was for me. And anyway, it's FUN!" That's it in a nutshell. In self-governance there is joy and ministry.

Adults play a valuable role in youth ministry. They provide continuity over the course of time. They give feedback, they offer perspective when things seem overwhelming. Like toddlers, the other stage of great independence and experimentation, youths need the freedom to make their own way. If adults lead the show, youth will be stunted in their growth and in their striving for independence. If adults are absent, youth can feel overwhelmed and can fail. Somewhere in the middle, between doing too much and doing too little, adults can offer adolescents helpful guidance. The presence of caring adults can be reassuring and stabilizing without taking away the independence that is the work of this age.

Adults must remember, however, that they should not seek to have their own emotional needs met by the youth. Adults working with youth need their own supportive peer group. This support is sometimes provided when adults work in teams. The appropriate adult role is a teeter-totter between too much and too little, complicated by the awareness that much is at stake.

Teens offer an interesting picture of the ideal advisor. They want someone who promotes spirituality and Unitarian Universalist values, upholds the democratic process, brings insight and ideas, encourages youth leadership, handles conflict effectively, is flexible yet maintains boundaries, tells the whole truth, does not mind being on equal standing with the youth, is confident and strong yet knows her/his personal limits, works well in teams with other adults, has her/his own peer group, has a sense of humor and vitality, doesn't wear a mask, trusts the youth to ask for help, shows good judgment, is a mentor and a good role model. Wow!

The power and success of youth ministry depends on the fact that youth offer one another emotional honesty and connection that adults simply cannot offer. The affirmations and honest emotional feedback they receive from each other is quite different from the understanding adults can provide. Youth ministry can be enriching, pleasurable, and life-affirming. When teens take advantage of the opportunity to learn about themselves while giving to others in a safe environment, lives can change.

~

Kathryn Deal is a marriage, family, and child counselor in West Los Angeles. Her specialties include working with families with deaf members. At the time of this writing, she was the Program Consultant focusing on high school age youth in the Pacific Southwest District.

Growth Through Diversity

Jean Wright Greenblatt,
Jennifer Hampshire, Hope Johnson,
Janice Marie Johnson, and Roberta Wallis

"commUnity" is our name. We are a multiethnic quintet of women from the Community Church of New York (in New York City) offering music, stories, and educational projects on diversity-related issues in an antiracist framework. We have developed musical programs, worship services, and workshops to bring our beliefs to the larger community. We started after an annual retreat for multicultural urban congregations at The Mountain in August 1993. "Building Bridges from Diversity to Community" was the theme of that meeting, and it inspired our future work.

The week itself was difficult. There was resistance, intolerance, and inappropriate behavior, along with the positive acknowledging of the importance of the work. At the end of the week, we friends decided to participate in the talent show. We selected a wonderful song, "Rosa," honoring Rosa Parks, women of color, and all women. The song was written by Libby Roderick of Alaska, a truly talented songwriter, singer, and activist. One of us signed as the others sang.

That song did it! At the end of our performance, many people wanted to hear it again. Several said, "Now I get it!" Now they understood this thing or that idea from this intense week around multiculturalism issues. Our small audience at The Mountain heard the message of love, pain, joy, justice, and injustice that is in that song. They saw a diverse group of women celebrating the message in unity—not in unison—with one sense of purpose. Unwittingly, happily, we'd found a safe vehicle for promoting our message. Suddenly we had a mission. We wanted the world to hear "Rosa" and other songs like it. We had witnessed the healing power of song and sign— "commUnity" was born!

An increasing emphasis on diversity and antiracism is emerging in Unitarian Universalism. We are urged to transform our congregations into more inclusive and diverse institutions. We hear the phrase "growth with diversity." We find the phrase uninspiring—as if the emphasis is really on growth, and diversity is an afterthought. "Let's grow our congregation, and oh by the way, wouldn't it be nice to throw in some diversity?" We prefer the phrase "growth *through* diversity." This places the emphasis on diversity, opening the door for a variety of ways to grow.

Let's examine some ways we grow in our churches. The obvious and commonly recognized are numerical growth and an increase in pledge income. But a church community can grow in other ways also. A congregation can learn to deal with conflict in an open and honest way. It can become more welcoming toward visitors, especially if those visitors look different or come from a culture unfamiliar to the congregation. The community also can grow through learning to talk about money in an open and concrete way, a subject more taboo in some places than sex or politics.

Congregations are deeply affected by the personal individual growth of their members, particularly the leaders. Look at your leaders as well as yourself. How well do you deal with ambiguity or the unknown? How uncomfortable are you talking to a stranger? How willing are you to put your ideals into action, to be involved in social action rather than to talk about it? How willing are you to support your church financially, to spend your money to support your faith? These sorts of individual growth will affect the entire church community and its capacity to grow more diverse.

Many churches still consider diversity to be about race, black and white. For many of us, this certainly is the first issue we need to face. But in our society today, there are many races and cultures besides African American and European American that should be considered in our efforts to be more inclusive. Some church members in our midst are not yet comfortable with gay and lesbian members. We can welcome many different kinds of families—the traditional family, the interracial family, the gay-parent family, and others. There is economic and social diversity: Unitarian Universalists still tend to be well-educated, middle- to upper-middle-class people, but we have an opportunity to expand our diversity by including folks who don't fall into those categories. Each congregation and its various groups can identify the diversities they can explore and embrace.

By intentionally welcoming people of different groups, we can grow *through* diversity. By fusing our efforts, we find ourselves growing whether we realize it or not, whether we intend to or not. When we sit at the table with someone from another culture or another race, and we learn to acknowledge, embrace, and learn from this person, we grow! When we learn to listen to others, to make room for process and for diversity of opinion and background, we grow! When we learn to live our beliefs, we grow!

Generally, Unitarian Universalists believe in the inherent worth and dignity of all people. But let's face the split between what we believe in our heads and how we live our lives. How many whites believe that they should include people of other races in our mostly white congregations, but have never had a person of another race or culture in their homes? How many of us believe in the inherent worth and dignity of gay and lesbian people, but can't accept homosexuality in our own families? How many white folks fight to keep hazardous waste facilities out of the neighborhood, but look the other way when they are placed in neighborhoods of people of color? How many of us believe in the interdependent web or in economic justice, but live a lifestyle that is contrary to principles of sustainable development? Yes, let's get honest. Diversity in its many forms offers us many ways of growing.

We members of "commUnity" at times have difficulty practicing what we preach. We intentionally work on this problem individually and collectively. We empower each other to be better, bigger than we are.

We are all very active members of our church because we believe that being active is important in one's church home. While we focus on racial, social, and environmental justice and the end to all forms of oppression, we are involved in other arenas, too. Among the five of us we have: a chair of our board of trustees; two former vice chairs; a treasurer; chair of the church council; chair of the nominating, diversity, finance, program and activities, and fund development committees; as well as former chairs of the social action and hospitality committees.

We are busy. We are stretched. But we observe how our work as members of our church is enhanced by our work as members of "commUnity." We notice that we now have a conceptual framework, to provoke dialogue and growth. The challenge excites us. We have fun together. Our meetings and rehearsals are often celebrations.

We consider ourselves to be a lay ministry. We participate in the empowerment of our laity through our worship services, workshops, forums, and special projects. We coordinate and facilitate group experiences that can be transforming. By sharing our struggles, our stories, our joys and concerns, we are taking folks on a journey, on the road with "commUnity."

How can we describe the honor and thrill that moved through us the first time we thought of our work as a lay ministry? Those magic words made the long hours, difficult trips, and the sometimes strange encounters worthwhile. As a group, commUnity processes each event we share. We discuss the ambivalent feelings and emotions, individually and collectively. We move into each other's space. We listen and learn.

We often use a one-person skit to dramatize the diversity within each of us and the commonality among us all. For example, one person can be a member of many groups: women, mothers, daughters, siblings, and more. At the same time, any one of us might fill several roles: homemaker, employer or employee, a member of several organizations. Each of us has good days, bad days, in-between days. One person might be a teacher, a student, at times both. We are truly multidimensional. We celebrate that!

Our personal diversity gives us a fantastic starting place for a common language. It enables us to acknowledge differences, no matter how alike we seem. This realization offers us a wonderful opportunity to welcome newness on our journey of discovery. Perhaps we all can participate in that moment of self-empowerment when we say in many voices, "This is what diversity is all about. This unity is what diversity can be—if we commit to the work that can make it happen."

As members of the human family, we believe we have the responsibility to welcome newness—new persons, new attitudes—into our lives. We feel called to examine our attitudes and assumptions about one another. We are called to examine how to welcome one another into our midst. We are called to challenge ourselves with what we discover about ourselves. We are called to act with a sense of urgency for social change. One person's oppression hurts us all, and one person's liberation helps us all. We move forward.

~

Jean Wright Greenblatt, Jennifer Hampshire, Hope Johnson, Janice Marie Johnson, and Roberta Wallis are members of the Community Church of New York in New York City. Between them they have held a variety of leadership roles: chair of the board of trustees, two former vice chairs, a treasurer, chair of the church council, and chairs of a number of church committees.

Working for the UUA

Kay Montgomery

I began working for the Unitarian Universalist Association in 1983 as a fundraising and financial consultant, fresh from Georgia, living alone for the first time in my life, my children back in Atlanta, living with their father for the first time in a decade—I missed them desperately. Boston was new to me; I was falling in love with it. My job was new to me; I wasn't at all sure that I hadn't oversold myself. Two years later I was appointed executive vice president. By this time I knew the UUA and had been to, probably, a third of our churches. Even by my own standards, I was a "success." But again I was afraid I had oversold myself. And both my sons were in the midst of a stormy adolescence.

For the first four years I was at the UUA, I had a secret. It was that sometimes I'd go home at night, eat, change to jeans, sneakers, and a sweatshirt, and then go back to work, timed so that I'd be there when our senior custodian, John Morris, came by to empty my wastebasket. We never talked very long, sometimes not at all. But every now and then he'd perch on the edge of my desk and we'd chat. He'd tell me about how things worked at our "shop." I'd tell him about what I was trying to figure out—about my life, about my job, about my children. He'd tell me about Lillian, his wife, and their plans for retirement. I was an ardent Unitarian Universalist; he was an ardent Seventh Day Adventist. Sometimes we talked about that. Once he told me about his early adulthood, about his struggles, about being "saved," and about how he saw life. A few years later, when my eldest, beloved son, Matt, was going through his own terrifying struggles, I was able to be present to him mostly because I remembered that John had been through something similar and had turned out to be—John.

When John Morris retired in 1987, I tried to tell him how much he had meant to me. I think he understood. He and I exchange notes sometimes. I saw him in 1993 in Charlotte, where he lives, and we talked for ten minutes or so. What I guess I will never know is whether John understands that he was my minister in those years. And what I guess I will never understand is how I knew to turn to him for ministry. Grace, I suspect.

Working for the Association can be hard. Sometimes the good folks in our congregations think of us as "them." And it's demanding and frustrating work, rich and challenging. It's one step removed from the purpose of our work—the support of healthy congregations where religion happens. We do so many different things: empty wastebaskets, balance budgets, hire and fire, buy hardware and software, send email and faxes and prepare spread-sheets, publish, talk to lawyers and accountants, meet with committees, write religious education curricula, teach and preach, plan events—workshops, seminars, General Assembly. We talk to the folks in our congregations, ministers and laypeople, give advice, often just listen. We run across one another—in the hallways, the elevator, the restrooms, in meetings designed to plan or worry, on Beacon Street in Boston, sometimes in airports, early in the morning, late at night or on the weekends, catching up. We talk on the phone to one another and meet across the continent in coffee shops and at restaurants where we plot and support one another, argue, dream, and scheme.

And sometimes, on our better days, we do ministry. Some of us are ordained, some are laypeople, some, as one friend said to me the other day—of me—"just a working stiff." But, on our better days, we do ministry—for one another and for the people in our congregations.

I grew up in working-class Detroit. Neither of my parents finished high school. My father quit school when he was twelve, went to work in the coal mines, and then spent most of his life working on an assembly line and bartending in what he called his "free time." My mother bore five children, made a home for all of us and for her angry and difficult mother-in-law, did a lot of volunteer work at our church, and, when she worked, worked as a maid. She was hunchbacked, funny, and deeply religious; the people in our neighborhood used to tell me that she was a saint. I think that, too. When my mother died there was a young woman at her funeral who I didn't know, tearful. She told me that my mother had worked in her home, after her own mother died when she was eight. Apparently, for four years, my mother, while ironing and cleaning, listened to the bereft young girl and loved her back to life. The young woman was a pediatrician, handsome and strong. This is ministry.

I wonder what my parents, now both long gone, would think of the work I do. It is so privileged. It's not a bit like an assembly line. It's harder in a way, and certainly tougher to measure and more difficult to talk about. We at the UUA try to change the world, to shake the very foundations, to make this bruised planet more gentle. We try to help our congregations be places of loving community that celebrate when a child is born and mourn when death comes, places where people are stretched to see their own part in the oppression of others, places that teach and nurture and where people learn what it is to be religious, where all of us are nudged into some kind of ministry. We are charged with being dreamers.

This is an amazing and complicated thing to be paid to do, this work of the church. The things we do here in Boston are so often prosaic, and yet more complicated because we bring our own human, imperfect selves to the venture of providing a life of the spirit for other people. Some days I marvel at whatever grace brought me to it. And some days I just do email.

We at headquarters come from very different places and for different reasons: ministers who are taking a break from parish life, or who feel called to minister to other ministers or to grow and change the Association; religious educators who yearn to create a new era of Sunday school curricula for a new generation of children and youth; laypeople (I am one) who realize that their greatest passions lie in the work of the church and are astonished and delighted to realize one day that the volunteer work that has been so satisfying can become their profession; young people right out of college who come to the Association for a few years before they begin graduate school, bringing laughter and fresh ideas; people who hope that working in a religious setting will bring more satisfaction than work in the secular world. Some settle in and stay, others find the distance between our goals and our reach just too hard to live with. Some go back to the world of churches or of business refreshed. Some leave angry and disillusioned.

But always, while we do this work, there is ministry. Our president, John Buehrens, knows it. He works, arguably, harder and longer than anyone I know. Sometimes he's hard to pin down. But I have learned that he will stop in his tracks and give me his total attention when I say, "I have a moral dilemma." John has an eye for the ministry of others, too. Last week he and I left the building late, tired from wrestling a recalcitrant budget into shape. Down the hall we saw our senior custodian, successor to my old friend John Morris. John nodded toward him and murmured to me, "You know, I love that guy. I suspect he's the most religious person in the place." John does ministry himself. Of course. But he honors it in others as well. And, like the rest of us, he needs it.

I am blessed every day with the ministry of my colleagues to me:

Mel, who for years now, with courage and compassion, has taught me about racism in my beloved religious home and in myself;

Bea, in whose nurturing presence, behind the closed doors of her office, I permit myself the occasional intemperate temper tantrum;

Makanah, who never misses an opportunity to let me know when I've done something well;

Bill, who's willing to argue me into the ground;

Steve, who, the day my brother died, simply showed up in my office with a voucher for a free airline trip, saying, "Maybe you or your kids could use this";

Myha, in the office next door, who told me once that she thought I had an old soul;

Bob, one of the gentlest people I know, who nevertheless is a truthteller ("Well," he once reluctantly opined, in response to my asking for feedback about a presentation I had made, "A for content; D for delivery");

and so many more, hundreds of people over the years, thousands of acts of ministry. Every day I am nurtured and ministered to and stretched, and every day I am astonished at the care, the passion for the work we do together.

The work of religion is demanding, hard work. Each day we try and each day we fail at something or another. The stakes are so high—a world transformed, a life enriched. We want and need so very much from one another. So here, in this religious bureaucracy, no one, so far as I know, questions who should be doing ministry. Everyone should.

My old friend and boss and mentor, David Rankin, minister of Fountain Street Church in Grand Rapids, Michigan, delivered a eulogy years ago for a woman we both knew and loved, a member and volunteer in the church where we both worked. In it, he said, "I remember an old professor in theological school. He once used the phrase 'minister to ministers.' He had just described all of the problems of the ministry, all of the hurt and the loneliness, and then he said: 'But there will often be a person in your church who will look after you, who will care for your needs. That person is a minister to ministers.'" And then David quoted this reading by an unknown author, called "Tribute to a Very Real Person."

People are of two kinds, and she
Was the kind I'd like to be.

Some preach their virtues, and a few
Express their lives by what they do;
That sort was she. No flowery phrase
Or glibly spoken word of praise
Won friends for her. She wasn't cheap
Or shallow, but her course ran deep,
And it was pure. You know the kind.
Not many in life you find
Whose deeds outrun their words so far
That more than what they seem, they are.

I used that reading at John Morris's retirement celebration. It described his ministry to the Association for twenty-five years and to me for four.

The language of shared ministry is fashionable right now. I like it. I think it accurately names and honors the best, highest-reaching interactions we have. But it would be an arrogant mistake to think that we had invented it. It is what people like John Morris and my mother and the woman David Rankin eulogized always did. It's what the best ministers have always urged their parishioners to do. And it is what those of us who are the bureaucrats of religion must do with one another and with ministers and with the laypeople in our congregations if our work is to succeed.

~

Kay Montgomery is the Executive Vice President of the Unitarian Universalist Association, the first woman and the first layperson to hold that position.

The Road to Better Communication

Frank Carl, Mary Hengstebeck, Jan Parsons, David Rohe, and Barbara Wise

For years our church stagnated at about 130 members. The size of our community should have supported a larger congregation. We had tried everything and none of it worked. We built a bigger sanctuary. Ministers came and went. Children's programs were emphasized and de-emphasized. We tried self-help seminars, discussion groups, and building rentals. How could we grow? What could we do to make our church more appealing?

Then two things happened. We became involved in the Unitarian Universalist Association's Decisions for Growth program, and part of that process called for learning how to resolve conflict in our church community. Then along came a real crisis to test our ability to cope. As a result of poor decision making concerning our ministry, we were in a major crisis. We worked closely with our district executive.

We five became the mediation panel. We are reasonably sure why two of us were chosen to be on the panel.

One of us was appointed by the board of directors of the church as a liaison between the panel and the board. She, as president-elect of the board, was the only panel member who was considered a leader at the time. One of us was appointed because she is a professional counselor. The logic for appointing the other three of us was not immediately obvious. Indeed, all three of us scored high on conflict avoidance when we were tested on our conflict resolution skills! Each of us joined the panel because we thought we would benefit by learning how to resolve conflicts. We were right. But only because we picked a good teacher.

Our first decision was whether we wanted to hire a professional. We hemmed and hawed—as we said, three of us were conflict-avoiders. By the time we were ready to decide, the situation between the minister and some church members had become volatile. The decision to ask for professional help was relatively easy under the circumstances. We had no choice.

The congregation breathed a collective sigh of relief when we recommended professional help. But what form would that help take, and how does one find a counselor for groups? Did this person need to be familiar with our church structure and philosophy? Could we hire a local person, someone we knew? Did we need someone to deal primarily with conflicts between individuals or someone to teach conflict management skills to the congregation? How long would we need the help?

The long list of unanswered questions froze us into

inaction. We were scared. Our approach was to involve the congregation as much as possible along the way, to bounce things off the people who were going to be affected by this process and to listen carefully to their responses. We recommended someone who was familiar with our church community but who was not local. Our inexperience and discomfort with conflict resolution actually may have worked in our favor. Since we were unsure, we sought help and guidance from the congregation. This atmosphere of inclusion helped to involve the congregants in the process.

We decided we wanted someone with considerable communication skills, someone who could identify the root sources of disagreements and deal with them, someone with experience in group dynamics and group communication. In short, a professional psychologist or social worker. We also decided it was important for the person to understand our church's philosophy and principles.

When we finished the groundwork and recommended a professional consultant, we thought that we were home free. Once we wrote the contract and got it signed, we thought our job was done. Fortunately our consultant didn't agree. Up to this point we had managed to do things well because we had some internal guidance and because we tried to involve everyone. Our consultant said that she could deal with the major interpersonal conflicts in the congregation on her monthly visits but we ourselves were going to have to be responsible for changing the quality of communication in the church. During her visits, our consultant agreed to teach us how to communicate effectively, and how to create a bond that sustains us and keeps us in close communication with each other.

It was important for the congregation to see that the problem issues were being dealt with. Obvious conflicts between congregants were identified for our consultant, who then made appointments with the parties involved, at first separately and then jointly to work out the process of conflict resolution. Looking back, we can see there were many things that needed to change in our church culture.

Our consultant led workshops for the congregants to learn skills in listening, speaking, confrontation, and ownership of one's feelings. As part of this experience, we learned to listen attentively to the speaker and to give feedback to be sure we understood not only what was said but also what was meant. We learned to express ourselves with "I" statements, telling the listener how we felt about something, particularly when the listener had a vested interest.

"I" statements indicate that you "own" the feelings that are elicited by the other person's action or statement. If you make no value judgement about the other person, but tell only how the other's action or words make you feel, the other person is less likely to take offense. For example, it is easier to accommodate someone who says, "I have trouble concentrating when you are whistling," instead of "Your whistling is awful, stop it." The first statement gets the desired results without hurting any feelings. The second may accomplish what you want, but it will invariably hurt feelings and probably harm later interactions.

When you own your own feelings, you are signifying

to the other person that your feelings are worth something to you. You are sharing your vulnerability, and in effect you invite the other person to respect your feelings. If that person is sensitive and caring, he/she will generally make an effort to accommodate your feelings. Fortunately, most people are sensitive and caring, especially in one-on-one situations and especially in churches.

The habit of owning and expressing feelings in this way can help all parties identify their priorities in the negotiation. Often a wide variety of apparently contradictory priorities can be accommodated, once known. Our mediation panel was approached several times by people who wanted us to fix a problem but didn't want to get involved. We learned to say no. Communication problems cannot be fixed without communication: the person asking for the solution to the problem needs to participate in the mediation process.

After five months the responsibility for changing the culture of communication fell to the mediation panel. Our consultant talked to us and prepared us for the challenge. She presented workshops to the congregation that were well attended and that prepared the congregation for the changes to come, and she dealt with the most immediate and intense conflicts. But between visits and after her contract expired much work was left to be done. We practiced our newly learned skills, and we reassured each other that we were becoming better communicators.

As members of the mediation panel, we hoped to set an example of good communication etiquette. We were asked to attend committee meetings as facilitators of appropriate communication. Eventually we realized that our main task was to work on our own communication habits. If we were successful in improving our own habits, we could set examples for others to follow, and this in turn would alter our culture of communication.

For small meetings of less than about fifteen people, we began a procedure called *check-in*. Each participant expresses his/her feelings of the moment. This procedure has two major advantages: it allows each participant to have the full attention of the group, and it offers the others some insight into the mood of the speaker. While these advantages may seem minor, they are significant in setting the mood for the meeting. And they help create a climate of ownership, in which participants feel they have been heard and have contributed to the meeting.

We also changed how we run our church gatherings, especially meetings. In the past, our meetings had been task-oriented. The convenor generally had an agenda and the conversation was usually focused on agenda items. Now our meetings emphasize process as well as task. After all, we are a church, we are a caring community. In our gatherings we now emphasize good communication and caring interactions in addition to task accomplishment.

We try to create an atmosphere in which all meeting participants are heard and no one is interrupted while speaking. Committee chairs are trained to support these communication protocols. This has stimulated an increased interest among the membership in day-to-day administrative matters. We've adopted a policy that allows sufficient communication before important decisions are made. This means we don't vote until everyone present understands the question and each person who wants to speak has been heard.

Probably the most difficult change was to learn to identify and confront divisive behaviors. These take many forms, but especially common are us-versus-them polarizations, in which congregations divide into enemies and friends, and third-party situations, in which person A has a problem with person B but complains to person C. One of these was sufficiently serious that professional intervention was necessary and the healing is still going on.

Because the habit of involving a third party is so common, we launched a congregation-wide educational effort. We took time to explain, individually and in groups, that when you have a problem with someone, the best person to help solve that problem is the person you have an issue with. It isn't productive to talk to someone who can't do anything about the problem. When we are approached with a complaint that doesn't involve us, we encourage the person to take the matter up with the individual involved. No matter how flattering it is to be confided in, we find it easy to resist this temptation once we recognize how our community suffers from this habit. Together, we committed ourselves to stopping third-party complaints.

Complainants are usually surprised by the reaction they get, especially when they remember to use their speaking skills and their "I" statements. Rarely is the conversation as difficult as the complainer feared, and the resolution of the problem is always worth the risk taken.

Not long ago our congregation was polarized over the issue of how we include our children in the worship service. Some members who were active in the children's program were convinced a significant number of members did not want children involved in the church at all.

To bring the problem into the open, we met with the leadership of the children's program. Our purpose was to facilitate communication between the children's program and the congregation. We wanted a balanced meeting, so we limited the mediation panel to three members, and expected the number of members of the children's program to be between six and eight.

Once the meeting began, the children's program director took control in spite of the fact that we had called the meeting. She read a statement that accused the church of being against children, then she tendered her resignation as director. Panel members were shocked and found themselves unprepared to handle a confrontation of this magnitude. The meeting ended after panel members told the director they would get back to her with a response once they had the opportunity to discuss her statement and the situation in general.

After several meetings and much discussions with our consultant, we recommended that an ad hoc committee be formed to address the best ways to involve the children in church activities. We also sent a letter to the director of children's programs, a letter both supportive and challenging. The letter adhered to principles of good communication: it commended the director for the many good things that she had done, and it said that individually and as a panel we disagreed with the dichotomy that she described in her statement.

Unfortunately, we have not been successful in reinvolving the director of children's programs since this conflict. She has remained upset. Sometimes it is not possible to satisfy the needs of an individual and provide for the health of the congregation. On the brighter side, we think our congregation learned much from this experience. We have learned that human interactions are extremely complex and that attempts to simplify them can damage communication and therefore resolution. Lines of communication, chains of authority, and a respect for congregational wishes are important to the health of the congregation. Any time any of these characteristics does not function maximally, the congregation suffers. With patience and hard work, we have improved the integration of our children into the church's overall program and begun the healing over the perceived polarization between the children's program and the rest of the congregation.

We've chosen to continue and sustain our work by training new mediation panel members to carry on the job of monitoring conflict and setting examples of good communication. For continuity, we included two members from the old panel. By extending the training to other members of the congregation and by increasing the circle of responsibility for setting good examples, we hope to create an atmosphere that fosters good communication and a culture of negotiation.

It is important to provide for continuity because any organization will tend to return to old and comfortable habits. For some of us, it requires a constant conscious effort to maintain the positive changes. As time rolls on, our new, healthier ways of communication will take root and become the norm. In the meantime, we must be watchful and remember all we've learned.

Conflict has two faces. One face stands for change and growth, energy and ideas for positive goals. The other face is destructive, and this is the face we fear. The ways we handle conflict determine whether or not it is constructive. Conflict hidden and unresolved can poison the best-laid plans. But conflict kept in the open and handled with skill can provide the impetus for necessary and lively growth. We know we have grown as individuals. Our church culture has changed. We are now healthy and poised for growth. Recently we entered the UUA Extension Ministry Program, and now we look forward to a bright future, a future not without problems but one in which we will have the communication skills to handle them.

∼

Frank Carl, Mary Hengstebeck, Jan Parsons, David Rohe, and Barbara Wise are members of the Unitarian Church of Augusta, Georgia. They have served their church in a vari-

ety of roles: board president, religious education committee member and teacher, and worship committee member. They are the founding members of the Mediation Panel.

Leadership in the Little
Old Church on the Green

Elisabeth McGregor

A little old church on the green set me on the path of becoming an active, ever-evolving Unitarian Universalist. In the last twenty years, that small New England church has evolved away from parochialism and toward fuller membership in the Unitarian Universalist community, away from a focus on preservation and toward a focus on mission, away from a pervading sense of limitation and toward a pervading sense of possibility. The renewal of our little old church is a story I hope we all can learn from.

In the late 1970s, the Sharon, Massachusetts, congregation numbered about thirty-five or forty, with attendance as low as ten on Sundays, plus a handful of children in the Sunday school. The meetinghouse cried out for major repairs and improvements and was a cause of constant concern. Sunday preaching, in a traditional service format, was provided by an underpaid, very part-time minister, unaffiliated with the Unitarian Universalist Association, whose main attention, understandably, went to his full-time job and family. The budget was small. Although there was vitality in the congregation's intellectual, religious, and social life, its institutional focus was on survival and preservation. There was more nostalgia for the past and desire simply to survive than there was vision and aspiration for the future. If we wanted to move out of the mode of mere survival, it was clear that we needed to change.

We asked, "Why are we here? Why shouldn't we just close down and merge with another congregation?" While the preservation of our heritage was a factor, the main issues were forward-looking: our desires for our children, ourselves, our community, and liberal religion. I remember the words of one long-term member: "If we close down, what will happen to the liberal religious witness in our community?" I was surprised to hear the term "religious witness" coming from one of the most ardent humanists in the congregation, but all of us recognized its validity. We chose to continue to exist because we had a mission to preach, teach, act, and live together the affirmations of liberal religion in a community that needed them. Now the question was how to do that most effectively.

We took part in a UUA self-study program, "Review and Renewal." One of the leaders dubbed us "the First Masochist Church of Sharon" for our habit of berating ourselves for our deficiencies and lapses from past status, rather than recognizing the vitality of our small religious education program and women's group, our adult activities and social action projects, our innovative lay-led worship services. We came to recognize that measuring ourselves by standards of the past was self-defeating and irrelevant. The standard that mattered now was one that looked forward, the standard of what we wanted to be and to accomplish.

We made hard decisions and took risks. We ended our part-time ministerial arrangement and became a lay-led fellowship for four years. During that time, we learned to organize and lead a rich, experimental variety of worship services, breaking with some of our stodgier traditions, and we learned to provide pastoral ministry to each other. In the absence of a professional minister, we were lay ministers by default, and the results included some remarkable leadership development. We accomplished some innovative and ambitious fundraising, and we invested heavily in a few key restoration projects which captured the congregation's enthusiasm and financial commitment. Gradually, we built up our programs and membership. From the experience of consciously being lay ministers, we gained a clearer understanding of what ministry meant, which we carried into our process of building back up to a professional ministry. We moved from a part-time student to a part-time minister to part-time interims, our efforts finally culminating in a successful application to the UUA's Extension Ministry program.

Today, with a congregation over 100, a church school over seventy, the once-empty sanctuary now bursting at the seams, and a full-time extension minister, the Sharon congregation has a new atmosphere. The difference goes beyond the increase in membership. Our attitude toward history has changed. While our history is still known and some traditions still honored, we talk less about our past and more about our present and future. We direct our energies inward less and outward more, with increased involvement in district and UUA affairs. Expanding our vision involved the hard work of many people. While various part-time ministers certainly advised and aided us on the path, we ourselves had to choose and travel the path from monument to mission.

There are particular joys and challenges to lay ministry in a church with lots of history. If the church building has escaped the curse (or perhaps blessing) of natural disasters, that history is often expressed visibly in a charming, antiquated building that demands constant care and attention like a crotchety old grandparent. There is the extensive mythology—heroes, colorful characters, occasional acknowledged rogues. The archives are full of old, brown-inked ledgers and letters that tell of past glory days, fights and schisms, ministers greater and lesser. Sometimes plaques and symbols are durably imbedded in the walls, so that each Sunday is a visible history lesson. The pews are almost surely uncomfortable antiques. There may be an old Communion set (and some discussion about how, or whether, to use it). Perhaps, as in Sharon, the meetinghouse is crowned with a Paul Revere bell, which gets treated with the liberal religious equivalent of the reverence due a saint's relics. Very likely there's a steeple, thrusting a peeling spire upward to claim its centrality in town, even though the demographic reality behind that claim has changed. The old church's history is not only written and engraved on tablets, it is also retold over coffee and from the pulpit—the living memory of how things were done two hundred years ago, twenty years ago, ten years ago.

An old church needs to preserve the relics and to keep the past alive. An imaginative and wise ministry of preservation can be a great gift to a congregation. One component of such a ministry is to care for the meetinghouse, the building itself. Of course, any congregation that owns a building must care for it, but this ministry takes on particular weight when the building is old, filled with the ghosts of spiritual ancestors, and recognized as a work of art and a historic site. The person who can coax heat from the old boiler and navigate generations of electrical wiring probably also knows the date the meetinghouse was built. The ministry of the meetinghouse and the ministry of preservation go hand-in-hand; sometimes the same person or group cares for both. When newcomers move into the circle of leadership, they often are expected to learn first about the history of the parish and its meetinghouse, and then about the finer points of Unitarian Universalism. The congregation probably has a written history, and if not, there are plenty of long-term members who can recite it. Few leaders of an old church, however recent their arrival, are totally untutored in their church's history.

This historical grounding, this attachment in time and place, is in many ways a blessing that can enrich the congregation's ministry. In the confusion and change of a rootless and transient society, the sense of belonging to a long-established institution and set of traditions can be gratifying. People settling in a new town often find that being a part of its old First Parish makes the town seem more like home, and the intermingling of town and church history gives the church a presence and status even among local people who are not members. Most important, the tangible presence of history reminds us of, and invites reflection on, the context of our own lives. There is a spiritual dimension to connecting ourselves with history, to "telling time in three directions," as David Nelson wrote in a meditation for the Unitarian Church of Sharon:

> The bang and the knock of steam pipes
> melt into the notes of Chopin.
> I count twenty panes over twenty,
> imperfect glass, distorting the bare limbs
> fluttering outside in a sharp March wind.
> The ceiling vaults in Neoclassic symmetry,
> White ridges, squares and swirls
> stamped before Douglas debated Lincoln.
>
> The timbers, cut at the local mill
> where water still runs fresh,
> link together in wooden pegs.
> Crisscrossed in sixty-watt darkness,
> the beams soar through the cavern
> to the clock tower where gears

the size of fists move hands to tell
time in three directions.

And above, the bell by Revere,
clapper worn uneven by the years.
Ringing for Appomattox, for VJ Day
and for the Vietnam Moratorium,
and on this day, rung by my two sons,
Tolled to bring us here to share
our histories.

The awareness and celebration of history can add another dimension to the sense of community felt in the
church, extending the church into time, both past and
future, as a historical community. We are more than the
sum of the individuals gathered at this moment. The whole
of us is greater than the parts, and the whole includes a
history, peopled with those whose gifts remain among us.
This sense of being part of a historical continuum can
strengthen the congregation's responsibility to care for and
pass on what has been entrusted to them. History can be
instructive. The ups and downs of the past can teach valuable lessons. The past can both remind and inspire us: "In
1856, our congregation stood against slavery; what are we
doing in 1996 to continue that tradition of standing against
racism?"

Belonging to an old church can also enhance appreciation of our Unitarian Universalist heritage. If Ballou or
Channing preached from your pulpit, if your congrega-

tion was involved in the schisms of the early 1800s that established Unitarianism, or if it was founded by one of the early Universalist missionaries, it is easier to make the history and heritage of liberal religion come alive and matter to your members. And history can be fun! People who can agree on little else can probably agree on historical celebration. The shared celebration can enhance the congregation's sense of unity and even promote healing in times of dissension.

There are drawbacks to this historical attachment, which lay leaders in old churches may recognize. The focus on the past can detract from attention to the present and future, and it can limit the vision of possibilities. "We have always done it this way" is heard in all congregations, but especially in older, more traditional churches with a strong sense of their history.

The historical focus can lead to complacency. "Olympia Brown was our minister. We've always been a forward-thinking, feminist congregation!" "We have a long history of social activism. We were a hotbed of Abolitionism and helped with the Underground Railroad!" Such history can be inspirational, or it can be an easy way out of dealing with the congregation's current responsibilities. There is always the temptation to idealize our congregation's past, to remember the wise and to forget the narrow and foolish, who may, in their own way, have as much to teach us.

The emphasis on history can be exclusive, even unwelcoming, in a religion that seeks to be inclusive. The history of our New England congregations is primarily white, northern European, and Protestant. The architecture, the traditional liturgical structure, and a thousand small traditions all reflect that background. But that is no longer who we are, or who we seek to be. A leader in my own church, of New York Jewish background, spoke of her discomfort in attending a little white church on the green that was so distinctively "Wasp" in its flavor, even though the actual ethnic composition of the congregation was quite diverse. The congregation's loving attention to history helped preserve elements of that "Waspiness." When we dwell too much on history that is monocultural, we run the risk of leaving out some of us. So the ministry of preservation has power for good and ill, and it carries real moral responsibilities.

The lay leader in an old church must help the congregation move from monument to mission. Old churches have a way of surviving, even when their natural life and usefulness have expired, but that doesn't mean they're healthy. Energy spent trying to hang on to a legacy is energy that is unavailable for the real work of the church. Preoccupation with the burden of survival and preservation can sap a congregation's vitality. First, when the members focus nostalgically on what they were, they invite depression, for often they have lost ground in size, wealth, and community status since their heyday, and comparison with the past is hardly likely to be cheering. Besides, focus on the past is likely to get in the way of taking risks and making changes to adapt to new conditions. The lament, "We used to have a huge Christmas fair, but we just can't get people to work on it anymore," doesn't make anyone feel very good. Preservationists sometimes forget to ask themselves: "Why are we preserving this? Should it be preserved?" History is valuable and instructive, but nostalgia can be both paralyzing and blinding. Seeing the church as a monument can make it hard to see it as a living body with an evolving mission that may need to depart radically from the past.

The basic challenge for leaders in an old church is one of vision, of turning the congregation's focus from its status as a monument to its mission as a religious body. The past should not be denigrated, but it cannot be worshiped. The task of the leadership is to get the congregation to stop asking, "How do we survive?" and to start asking, "What is our mission? What do we most want to accomplish?"

These were the vital questions I heard when I attended a recent anniversary at the Universalist Unitarian Church of Brockton, Massachusetts. The congregation was celebrating two anniversaries: the merger of the local Universalists and Unitarians (eight years before the denominational merger) and the erection of a new building now forty years old. Today Brockton is an impoverished and declining New England mill city that has undergone tremendous demographic and social change in recent years. The congregation has aged and dwindled in size and resources during the forty-year lifetime of its fine, large building. But not to dwell in nostalgia, the celebration focused on the future, on the mission of a church in a city that desperately needs its presence and help.

After reflecting on what they were called to do, the Brockton congregation recently decided that they must invest money and energy in the Brockton Interfaith Council, which runs an ambitious program of local political and social action. They sought UUA funds to help build a public playground nearby. At the service, talk did not neglect the past or deny the realities of decline in the present, but its focus was on the church's mission now and in the future. The recent history of the Universalist Unitarian Church of Brockton is one of beginning the movement from monument to mission.

Sometimes the church should not survive in its present state. Perhaps it should move from its historic site, or merge with another congregation, or even dissolve and put its resources to better use. Scattered all over New England are churches that have refused to face this hard conclusion, preferring to resign themselves to preservationist irrelevance in their community. Others have taken these steps. Fortunately, when nostalgia is repudiated and a focus on mission happens soon enough, such drastic change is unnecessary.

Another problem of old churches is localism. Old churches are often notoriously turf-bound, geographically and conceptually. In an age of highways and modern communication, traveling a dozen miles or crossing a town line should not be a barrier to any voluntary activity. But that barrier still exists in the minds of many New England congregations. The Unitarian Church of Sharon was progressive enough to call a woman minister in the early 1890s, but it took nearly another hundred years before it elected a parish president who did not come from Sharon.

Old churches date back to the days when families stayed put in a town and rarely crossed its boundaries. Most historically Unitarian churches in New England were political entities whose identity and governance were closely intertwined with that of the town. They were, and often still are, the First Parish of Our Town. They existed as congregations first. Unitarianism came later.

There are positive aspects to historically grounded localism. A strong local identity can foster strong community responsibility, which is an excellent part of a church's mission. It can integrate members' church lives with their lives as community citizens. But leaders of localist congregations need to challenge the tendency to draw the mental boundaries of community too narrowly, stopping at town lines. Why should we care only about the welfare of our town? Why should we invite only those from our town into our church community? This anachronism ignores the increasingly regional nature of our economic and cultural communities and the increased mobility of the average person, who may travel thirty miles to work every day and live in several states in a lifetime. Limited by a narrow focus on their own town, churches may fail to reach out to those from nearby towns, and even if they do, they may fail to integrate them fully into a church life that is too town-based. They may miss opportunities for community service that go beyond their self-defined borders. In my church in Sharon, we are just beginning to address this problem, under gentle prompting from the growing number of newer members who live outside Sharon. Lay leaders need to foster and hasten this evolution from local to regional thinking.

When Unitarian Universalist churches are geographically close together, how do they deal with the unspoken suspicion, envy, and competition that may lurk among them? This turf war, a mentality of scarcity, feeds the fear that the neighbor church will steal "our" people, and the belief that if the neighbor church does well, our church will suffer. This suspicion, combined with a locally bound identity, hinders a whole range of outreach and cooperation efforts that could greatly enhance the vitality of Unitarian Universalism in general.

We in old churches must nurture a vision of ourselves as Unitarian Universalists. Moving beyond the boundaries of our town and our church, we must loosen our hold on the past. Then we will see our neighboring Unitarian Universalist churches as partners in a common endeavor. We will recognize that some people who come to our door might be happier in the nearby Unitarian Universalist church whose interests and style of worship better match their own. The strength of that neighbor church is very much in our practical interest.

In addition, most members now in our churches will not stay for life. We need to think about training Unitarian Universalist leaders, not just leaders for our own church. Given what we know of economies of scale and the value of diverse input, why should we design and run programs by and for ourselves, when we could share them with our neighbors? Let's invest more often in cluster and district programming and in shared projects. It's vital for leaders who participate in conferences, workshops, and the General Assembly to share their experience and knowledge with their congregation. Anything we do together as Unitarian Universalists helps to break down the barriers of isolation and parochialism, and it often infuses new ideas and energy into congregations that have become stale on their own. At the delightful 1995 New England Gathering in Worcester, Massachusetts, I met the president of a neighbor church who had never before been to a district event. At this meeting he was enthused, inspired—and he wondered why he'd never done this before.

Lately, I've seen evidence in the Ballou Channing District that church leaders are increasingly transcending the local focus. For instance, cluster programming is growing. One dramatic example is the current cooperation between the Chatham and Brewster congregations, which lie twenty miles apart on Cape Cod. The Chatham fellowship, a lay-led group of some forty members, mostly retired, meeting in rented space, had just successfully raised enough money to hire a part-time minister. Suddenly a church building in town became available. An internal fundraising campaign, though successful, could not meet the full amount needed for a mortgage. So the Chatham congregation approached the much larger Brewster church for help. By congregational vote, Brewster agreed to give the Chatham congregation $10,000 and to loan them another

$60,000 toward the cost of ministry, plus offer them program support and assistance in starting a Sunday school. The crowded Brewster congregation also encouraged members who wanted to belong to a smaller church to join or at least attend the Chatham church. By early October, an enlarged Chatham congregation with a new religious education program was holding services in its new building.

And finally, the old church must contend with its building. In my district there aren't many new buildings. The historic old building, while it may be handsome, is likely to have inadequate parking, steep stairways, antiquated plumbing and heating, hard pews, peeling lead paint, a precarious steeple, building code violations, a damp basement, dark little Sunday school rooms, and an old-fashioned kitchen. Besides being costly, inconvenient, and exasperating, these buildings are also works of art and rich repositories of history. They are a focal point for community life and identity, and they are loved. The trick for church leaders is how to appreciate and care for their building without letting it run the congregation's life. When the building becomes an object of worship rather than a place of worship, the congregation has what I call the "edifice complex." When the cost of building maintenance squeezes vital programs out of the budget, the congregation is in trouble. The edifice complex is a problem that falls squarely on the shoulders of the laity, not the minister.

Symptoms of the complex can be heard at committee meetings. "We can't have the children upstairs because it will hurt the furniture." "Those banners will damage the plaster." "We can't afford to pay our religious education director, and we can't afford to pay our fair share to the Association, because we have an expensive old building to maintain." This is the edifice complex.

The remedy for this ailment requires that the leadership restore the building to its proper place in the church's mission. Our buildings serve the mission of the congregation, not the other way around. A congregation like the First Parish of Brewster hasn't tripled in size because of its fine old building, but rather in spite of the building's limits (which force the congregation to hold three services and Sunday school sessions every week). The congregation grew because it was committed to its mission and programs and didn't allow the building to become an excuse for stunting them. Now, to meet the needs of its programs, the Brewster congregation is considering options for building expansion that include moving out of the old building. This step is almost unthinkable for a church focused on survival and preservation, but not so scary for a church focused on its mission.

Lay leaders need to counter the plea of building-induced poverty. While our meetinghouse in Sharon has faced more than its share of costly repairs and has its shabby spots, our president has presented the case in a positive light: "At least we own the building, it meets our needs reasonably well, and the mortgage is paid off. Think of how many Unitarian Universalist churches aren't in as good a position." He compared our financial situation, supporting an aging building, to that of the Unitarian

Universalist Fellowship in Falmouth, Massachusetts, which has taken on a huge debt to build its first meetinghouse. If Falmouth could always manage to support its program and pay its fair share to the UUA, we certainly could. Perception is all-important, and lay leaders are vital in modeling and shaping a congregation's perception of itself. They can see themselves as poor and cursed with the burden of an old building, or they can see themselves as rich and blessed with a good old home; either position sets a tone and helps establish an energy level for the congregation's activities.

In Sharon, we haven't cured the edifice complex, but we've come a long way toward taming it. In response to serious crises (a steeple listing dangerously, termites eating out the floor and beams), we found creative and enjoyable ways to raise funds, such as presenting theatrical productions. To draw contributions and involvement from local sources outside the church, we created a separate organization, the Friends of the Meetinghouse, which by bylaw includes non-church members, to oversee historic preservation. They administer a Meetinghouse Preservation Fund, to which the church must apply to obtain funds for projects involving historic features of the building. To meet ongoing needs such as painting, we have established a prioritized schedule for upcoming years. Each year, we set aside a small percentage of the budget in a Capital Reserve Fund, to save up for major projects.

Now we don't say, "Why should we be stuck maintaining a museum?" Instead we say, "We've been given this space as a home and a trust to keep, and we're lucky to have it." We've made peace with the things we can't fix and plan to fix the things we can. We've learned to live with some shabby spots, knowing we'll get to them when we can. We trust the people we've delegated to the tasks.

Of course, like most New England congregations in old edifices, we still put many hours of volunteer time and plenty of money into the building. But in committees and parish meetings, we spend less time talking about the building than we used to, largely because we have other things to talk about. Lately, congregational talk about the building is more likely to be about future space needs than about problems of repair and preservation. With a shift in orientation from the past to the future, from preservation to mission, we have set our beloved old building, like our long history, into a more healthful perspective.

In the growth and evolution of the Sharon church, I see the sort of change that is within the reach of all the little old churches—if their leaders choose to pursue it. The change begins with a vision that, in the words of the old hymn, "reveres the past, but trusts the dawning future more." This vision can be inspired and cultivated by a professional minister, but it also must be embraced, spoken, and modeled by the lay leaders of the congregation, or it will not take hold. It is the ministry of the lay leaders to help their congregations take that chance and make that reach. In the coming century, I see a greening of the little old churches on the green, if only they will re-envision themselves.

~

Elisabeth McGregor is a Trustee of the UUA from the Ballou Channing District. She is a twenty-two-year member of the Unitarian Church in Sharon, Massachusetts, where she has held various offices. She lives in Sharon with her family and teaches English at Stonehill College.